MW00587481

GAZING ON HIS FACE

Gazing on His Face

A Christ-Centered Spirituality

Robin Ryan, CP

Paulist Press
New York / Mahwah, NJ

Scripture texts in this work are taken from the *New American Bible, revised edition* © 2010, 1991, 1986, 1970 Confraternity of Christian Doctrine, Washington, D.C. and are used by permission of the copyright owner. All Rights Reserved. No part of the New American Bible may be reproduced in any form without permission in writing from the copyright owner.

Cover image by Bernardo Ramonfaur / Shutterstock.com
Cover design by Sharyn Banks
Book design by Lynn Else

Copyright © 2020 by Robin Ryan, CP

All rights reserved. No part of this publication may be reproduced, stored in a retrieval system, or transmitted in any form or by any means, electronic, mechanical, photocopying, recording, scanning, or otherwise, without either the prior written permission of the Publisher, or authorization through payment of the appropriate per-copy fee to the Copyright Clearance Center, Inc., www .copyright.com. Requests to the Publisher for permission should be addressed to the Permissions Department, Paulist Press, permissions@paulistpress.com.

Library of Congress Cataloging-in-Publication Data
Names: Ryan, Robin, author.
Title: Gazing on his face : a Christ-centered spirituality / Robin Ryan, CP.
Description: New York : Paulist Press, 2020. | Includes bibliographical references. | Summary: "The mystery of Christ's person and saving work is explored by a series of reflections on a number of titles for Christ that have been ascribed to him in the Christian tradition"— Provided by publisher.
Identifiers: LCCN 2019044791 (print) | LCCN 2019044792 (ebook) | ISBN 9780809155026 (paperback) | ISBN 9781587689024 (ebook)
Subjects: LCSH: Spirituality—Catholic Church. | Jesus Christ—Name.
Classification: LCC BX2350.65 .R925 2020 (print) | LCC BX2350.65 (ebook) | DDC 232—dc23
LC record available at https://lccn.loc.gov/2019044791
LC ebook record available at https://lccn.loc.gov/2019044792

ISBN 978-0-8091-5502-6 (paperback)
ISBN 978-1-58768-902-4 (e-book)

Published by Paulist Press
997 Macarthur Boulevard
Mahwah, New Jersey 07430
www.paulistpress.com

Printed and bound in the
United States of America

To My Passionist Brothers
In Gratitude for Their Support along the Way

Contents

Preface

As a professor of systematic theology, I have taught courses in Christology at the graduate level for twenty-five years. Christology is that dimension of Christian theology that studies the person and the saving work of Jesus Christ. In Christology students explore the Old Testament background for faith in Jesus, the distinct portraits of Jesus given by the four Gospel writers, the thought of Paul on God's redemptive action in and through Christ, and the wealth of reflections on Christ given by the other authors of the New Testament. The study of Christology also entails consideration of the development of doctrine about Christ in the history of the church, the work of classical theologians like Thomas Aquinas and Bonaventure, the thought of spiritual masters like Julian of Norwich and Teresa of Avila, as well as the reflections on the person and work of Christ offered by contemporary theologians from a rich variety of contexts.

Two thinkers have enriched my understanding and appreciation of Jesus in a particular way. The first is the twentieth-century German theologian Karl Rahner (1904–84). Rahner has authored many essays and books on the academic study of Christ, especially his well-known work *Foundations of Christian Faith*.[1] Rahner's lengthy section on Christology in *Foundations* is a rigorous treatment of the church's doctrine about Christ as well as a compelling articulation of his own theological perspective on Christ. But what is particularly intriguing about Rahner's Christology is that he includes a section on personal relationship with Jesus Christ as an integral part of his systematic Christology. Rahner admits that in the "average dogmatic theology" this topic is not usually covered.[2] But he thinks that it is essential to Christology, precisely because Christianity understands itself as a process of entering into and developing a personal relationship with Jesus Christ.

Rahner proceeds to explore the meaning of this personal relationship. It is not something that is fully attained or realized at any single moment in one's life. It is a relationship that must be continually renewed through encountering Christ in the sacraments, prayerful study of the Christian Scriptures, and the effort to put into concrete practice in one's life the teaching of the gospel. It is always a process that calls for further growth. In this practice, Christians are invited to entrust their lives and their very selves to God through Jesus, who has made God personal and concrete in human history.

Rahner reminds us that the humanity of Jesus was not left behind in his resurrection. Rather, Jesus's humanity was raised up, and it "continues to exist forever as the reality of the eternal Logos [Word of God] himself."[3] Thus, Christ's risen humanity continues to mediate to us the reality of God. This means that in building a loving relationship with the human Jesus, the Christian is embracing, and is embraced by, the living God.

Living the Christian life does not entail a "cookie cutter" discipleship. Rather, each Christian is invited into a unique relationship with Jesus that reflects the context of her or his life. Rahner asserts "that there can be and is a unique relationship between each individual and Jesus Christ, and that in the individual Christian there must be a quite personal and intimate love for Jesus Christ."[4] Such a personal love for Christ is inseparably united with a genuine love of neighbor. Love of neighbor, in fact, is a prerequisite for love of Jesus. At the same time, our love of our fellow women and men grows through our love of Jesus, since "it is only in a loving relationship with Jesus that we conceive the possibilities of love

for neighbor that otherwise we should simply not hold to be fea-
sible, but which present themselves nonetheless wherever we sub-
sume our neighbor in our love for Jesus because he or she is Jesus'
brother or sister."[5] In other words, personal love of Jesus impels and
inspires creative, concrete love of our neighbors.

Rahner portrays this call to a personal relationship with Jesus
in a very down-to-earth way in an essay that he wrote. He recalls
a conversation he had with a Protestant theologian in which he
[Rahner] said, "Yes, you see, you're actually only really dealing
with Jesus when you throw your arms around him and realize
right down to the bottom of your being that this is something you
can do today."[6] Believers can still do this today because in his resurrection Jesus has attained a presence throughout the universe,
and his risen humanity remains the abiding mediation of God.
Thus, for Rahner an indispensable dimension of the life of the
Christian is a unique, loving relationship with the person of Jesus,
who is indescribably close to each one of us.

The second thinker who has influenced my reflection on
the person and work of Jesus Christ is Pope Francis. He has consistently spoken of Jesus as the face of the Father's mercy. And he
has exhorted every Christian to spend time gazing on the face of
Jesus. In a section on the necessity of constant prayer that is found
in his apostolic exhortation on the Call to Holiness in Today's
World, Francis speaks of contemplation of the face of Jesus:

> We need to remember that "contemplation of the
> face of Jesus, died and risen, restores our humanity,
> even when it has been broken by the troubles of life
> or marred by sin. We must not domesticate the power
> of the face of Christ." So let me ask you: Are there
> moments when you place yourself quietly in the Lord's
> presence, when you calmly spend time with him,
> when you bask in his gaze? Do you let his fire inflame
> your heart? Unless you let him warm you more and

more with his love and tenderness, you will not catch fire. (*Gaudete et Exsultate* 151)[7]

For Francis, then, contemplation of the face of Jesus restores our humanity, especially when our humanity has been wounded by our own failures or by the sufferings we have endured. The face of Christ has power—healing and renewing power. Thus, every believer is invited to spend time with the living Jesus, to sit quietly in his presence, to bask in his gaze. It is in and through such moments that we "catch fire" and are empowered to live as energetic disciples of Jesus, continuing his mission in the world. It is through such contemplation that we are impelled to engage in the praxis of the reign of God that Jesus proclaimed and made present.

A Christ-Centered Spirituality

This book is grounded in the tradition of Christology, but it is an effort to develop a Christ-centered *spirituality*. Spirituality is a discipline within theology, but more fundamentally the word speaks to an experience and a way of life. Theologian Joann Wolski Conn says that for Christians spirituality "means one's entire life as understood, felt, imagined, and decided upon in relationship to God, in Christ Jesus, empowered by the Spirit."[8] Thus, a Christ-centered spirituality must speak to our entire life—our relationships with God, other people, creation, and self. It must address both the personal and the social dimensions of life. This spirituality must inform our understanding and our feelings, relating both to the intellectual and affective aspects of being human. And it must inspire our imagination—the possibilities that we envision, as well as our decisions—the concrete choices we make that give direction to our lives.

Though Jesus Christ stands at the very center of all Christian belief and thought, the approach to Christian spirituality that I adopt in this book is only one possible way of articulating a Christian spirituality. Other ways of proceeding give rise to a Trinitarian focus on spirituality, a Spirit-centered (pneumatological) spirituality, a liberationist spirituality, a feminist spirituality, an ecological spirituality, among many others. Each of these approaches seeks to integrate the person and work of Jesus Christ into its elaboration of what it means to live the Christian life.

The person and the work of Jesus Christ are one of the central mysteries of the Christian faith. This mystery reflects our experience of the self-communication of God in human history in the most personal of ways. It is ultimately about God's gracious presence and action in history. Though we can grow in our understanding of this mystery through prayerful reflection and study, we will never "wrap our minds" around this mystery, which is an object of faith. Therefore, no book on Christian spirituality can fully explore and articulate the mystery of Jesus Christ. In many ways, we can only scratch the surface.

In this book, I approach the mystery of Christ's person and saving work by reflecting on a number of titles for Christ that have been ascribed to him in the Christian tradition. These include the following: friend, healing presence of God, caller of disciples, Bread of Life, Good Shepherd, Priest, Brother, Prince of Peace, and Good Samaritan. Each title can serve as a window through which we can contemplate the mystery of the one whom Christians confess to be Lord and Savior. Reflection on the meaning of these christological titles can enrich our understanding of a Christ-centered spirituality for today.

Gazing on Beauty

I invite the reader to do what Pope Francis suggests in his exhortation on the call to holiness: to contemplate the face of Jesus. Francis tells us that there is power in the face of Christ.

That is certainly true. But one also finds beauty in that face—exquisite beauty. Theologian Gerald O'Collins, who has authored numerous books on Christology, reflects on the beauty of Christ in his book *Jesus: A Portrait*.[9] He cites a famous homily of Saint Augustine (354–430) on Psalm 45. This Hebrew psalm originally celebrated a royal marriage in Israel. But Christian thinkers from the time of the early church have interpreted it to refer to the relationship between Christ the Bridegroom and his church, the Bride. Envisioning Christ to be the fulfillment of the Psalmist's description of the king, Augustine lauds his beauty:

> He was beautiful in heaven, then, and beautiful on earth: beautiful in the womb and beautiful in his parents' arms. He was beautiful in his miracles but just as beautiful under the scourges, beautiful as he invited us to life, but beautiful too in not shrinking from death, beautiful in laying down his life and beautiful in taking it up again, beautiful on the cross, beautiful in the tomb, and beautiful in heaven.[10]

O'Collins observes that when Augustine claims that Christ was "just as beautiful under the scourge," we are compelled to acknowledge "how the crucified Jesus in a radically subversive way challenges all the normal indices of beauty."[11] Even in the most repulsive moments of his passion, as Jesus is being tortured to death, believers can contemplate the supreme beauty of infinite, self-giving love. And they are "summoned to recognize beauty in the weak and suffering men and women with whom Christ identifies himself."[12] It is the faithful, steadfast love radiated in the face of Christ that has attracted countless men and women through the centuries, beginning with his public ministry and the call of his first disciples.

O'Collins refers to a famous painting by the Italian artist Caravaggio (1571–1610), *The Calling of Matthew*, which is kept in the Church of Saint Louis in Rome. It depicts Jesus pointing at Matthew, as Matthew is busily at work at his tax collector's post. In response, Matthew points at himself as if to say, "Do you really mean me?" Caravaggio's blend of light and shadows in this painting is remarkable. O'Collins reflects on this masterpiece in these words: "The look on the face of the beautiful Christ calls Matthew to new life. In turn, the light on the face of Matthew shows that he has recognized the beautiful Light of God who has come into the world (John 1:9; 9:5). The divine face and the human face meet in a moment of creation and recreation."[13]

It is my hope that in reading and praying with the chapters of this book, readers will be drawn to contemplate the beautiful face of Christ and, in so doing, will experience a call to new life. By reflecting on the mystery of Christ through the "windows" of traditional christological titles, our own faces and the face of Christ can meet in a moment of creation and recreation.

Chapter 1

Christt the Friend

Building Friendship with Christ

In the introduction to this book, I took note of Pope Francis's observation that contemplation of the face of Jesus restores our humanity. The first aspect of the mystery of Jesus Christ that I will explore resonates with a deeply human experience — the gift of friendship. Friendship is one of the greatest treasures in our lives. We work hard to build strong friendships and to nurture those relationships through the years. We celebrate those friendships in a rich variety of ways, and we grieve deeply when we lose a friend. As we grow older and look back on our lives, we recognize that having good friends is more important than most of the other treasures we have accumulated or achievements we have realized.

In a well-known passage from the Gospel of John, Jesus invites his disciples to live in friendship with him:

> As the Father loves me, so I also love you. Remain in my love. If you keep my commandments, you will remain in my love, just as I have kept my Father's commandments and remain in his love. I have told

1

you this so that my joy may be in you and your joy may be complete. This is my commandment: love one another as I love you. No one has greater love than this, to lay down one's life for one's friends. You are my friends if you do what I command you. I no longer call you slaves, because a slave does not know what his master is doing. I have called you friends, because I have told you everything I have heard from my Father. (John 15:9–15)

This passage is part of the lengthy farewell discourse in the Gospel of John. This discourse is set within the context of Jesus's final meal with his disciples before the "hour" of his passion. At that meal, he assumes the role of a servant and washes the feet of his disciples. Then he offers his "last will and testament," in which he instructs his disciples about their relationship with him and their mission in the world.

Through a rich mosaic of images, the Gospel of John depicts Jesus as the source of life and fruitfulness for all people. Those images are very familiar to us. They include Living Water, Bread of Life, Light of the World, Good Shepherd, and more. This passage from the fifteenth chapter of the Gospel of John follows Jesus's words that employ another familiar image, that of the vine: "I am the true vine, and my Father is the vine grower" (John 15:1). The image of the vine/vineyard is evoked in the Old Testament to depict the relationship of the people of Israel to God, with whom they had entered into a covenant bond (see Isa 5:1–7; Ps 80:9–17). In the Gospel, it is a symbol that expresses the closeness of communion with Jesus. A vine and its branches are intertwined. Just so, Jesus is the source of life for those who "remain" in him. The word *remain* (*menein* in Greek) reflects an important theme in the Gospel of John. Disciples must "remain" or "abide" in Jesus. This section of the Gospel speaks about *connection*—about the call to every disciple to strengthen her or his connection with Jesus. Without this vital connection, our discipleship loses its nourishment and its very life. Today we live in a world where people are almost desperate to establish connections. Witness the voluminous use of social networks. Young and old go to the greatest lengths to stay connected with one another. Long before these Internet innovations, the Gospel of John was instructing readers about the importance of believers strengthening their connections with Christ and with one another.

It is in the context of Jesus's discourse about the vine and the branches that we are introduced to the theme of friendship. Jesus seems to surprise his disciples by calling them "friends." You can almost picture the disciples as taken aback at these words of Jesus. They are no longer to think of themselves as slaves, servants, apprentices, or merely students, but as the friends of Jesus. He calls them friends because he has communicated to them all that he has heard from his Father. Just as Jesus shares life with his Father, so he invites his disciples to a sharing of life that is friendship. This is a crucial moment in the narrative of the Gospel, and it is a very significant invitation to disciples of every time and place.

In the narrative of the Gospel of John, this scene is set within the context of the "hour" of Jesus—that critical time in the journey of Jesus that is looming. It is the hour of Jesus's passion—of his betrayal and death, but also of his glorification. At the beginning of the farewell discourse, Jesus had told his disciples, "Do not let your hearts be troubled" (John 14:1). But this must have been a very troubling time for all of them. We can imagine ourselves sitting at table with Jesus at this moment. The atmosphere must have been charged with uncertainty and intense anxiety, as Jesus's disciples wondered what would happen to him and what would happen to them, his followers. It must have been clear that the net was closing in upon them. At such times, what is most important in life becomes clarified; everything becomes limpidly clear. It is in that tense atmosphere that Jesus defines the character of his friendship-love by proclaiming what he will soon do: "No one has greater love than this, to lay down one's life for one's friends" (John 15:13). It is the love of God incarnated in Jesus that comes first in the Gospel. Grace always precedes our response, and grace makes our response to God's love possible. It is the love of God poured out in Jesus that elicits the response of his disciples, and here it is shown to be a love to the very end—a love that goes to the greatest lengths. The offer of friendship by Jesus is a gift; it is not something earned or deserved, but is a gift meant to evoke a response in us. It all begins with a gift.

So often in our lives we see the truth of the Scriptures illumined in the lives of people whom we encounter. When I was a freshman in college in Richmond, Virginia, I engaged in some volunteer service in a poor, rooming house part of the city. It was there that I met a man named George. At the time George was in his fifties and lived by himself in the drab front room of a run-down house. George was legally blind and suffered from severe epilepsy. The physicians at the public clinic that he visited had difficulty finding the right blend of medications to control his seizures. His epilepsy had been aggravated years before when, while he was selling newspapers on a downtown street corner, someone hit him over the head with a metal pipe and stole the fifteen dollars he had in his pocket. George also had some cognitive deficits, though he had greater intellectual acumen than most people realized. He barely survived on public assistance, struggling at the end of every month to make it until his check arrived in the mail.

I soon realized that George was a friend of Christ; he was one of Christ's closest friends. When I would knock on the door of his room, I would often find him sitting on his bed reading from a large braille volume of the New Testament. Each Sunday, George would put on his cleanest pair of pants and best suitcoat and take the bus downtown to Centenary Methodist Church, where he worshiped. He once told me, with a deep sense of pride and satisfaction, that years before he had been able to contribute fifty dollars to the church fund to help finance a light that hung over the pulpit where the Word of God was proclaimed. George had a rather cryptic way of speaking; when he spoke of Jesus, he referred to him simply as "The Savior." Sometimes he would tell me about the in-depth conversations he had with The Savior.

I was nineteen years old at the time, trying to figure out my place in life and discern my vocation. Raised in a more privileged part of the city, I had never had a friend like George. And we remained friends through the years even after I left Richmond and was ordained a Passionist priest, until George finally died in a nursing home. Though I did not have the vocabulary to express it at the time, George showed me something about what it means to "remain" in Christ. And he taught me—the college student—about the invitation to live as a friend of Christ.

Friendship in the Christian Tradition

The theme of friendship has been explored and developed by towering Christian thinkers. In the thirteenth century, Saint Thomas Aquinas, building on the philosophy of Aristotle, described the theological virtue of charity as friendship with God, citing John 15 in his explanation.[1] Saint Teresa of Avila, writing in the sixteenth century, was also deeply influenced by the gospel teaching about friendship with Christ. At twenty years old, Teresa entered the Carmelite monastery, where she endured serious illnesses that almost took her life on more than one occasion. After she recovered, she lived a religious life that she felt was neither satisfying nor particularly fervent. But when she was thirty-nine years old, she had a powerful experience of God while praying before a statue of the scourged Christ. From that time on, she resolved to live a life of deeper friendship with Christ.

In her autobiography, her *Life*, Teresa offers what may be the best description of prayer ever given. Pope Francis cited her definition in his 2018 apostolic exhortation On the Call to Holiness (*Gaudete et Exsultate* 149). In this passage she is describing mental prayer, but her definition applies, I believe, to personal prayer in general. Teresa writes, "For mental prayer in my opinion is nothing else than an intimate sharing between friends; it means taking time frequently to be alone with Him who we know loves us."[2] Teresa sets the meaning of prayer within the context of friendship with God. On the one hand, her description is simple and straightforward, but on the other hand, there is a depth to it that invites ongoing reflection. It certainly echoes the words of Jesus in the farewell discourse of the Gospel of John. Pope Francis says about Teresa's description of prayer, "I would insist that this is true not only for the privileged few but for all of us" (*Gaudete et Exsultate* 149).

Further along in her autobiography, Teresa speaks of her experience of gazing on the sacred humanity of Jesus. Some of the spiritual experts of her day taught that, once a person reaches an advanced stage on the path to union with God, he or she must leave behind consideration of all created things, even the humanity of Jesus. From her own experience of prayer, Teresa contested this teaching, counseling her readers to spend time engaging the human Jesus in reflection and prayer. This is the Jesus whom Teresa addresses as "friend." She writes, "Whoever lives in the presence of so good a friend and excellent a leader, who went ahead of us to be the first to suffer, can endure all things. The Lord helps us, strengthens us, and never fails: He is true friend."[3] For Teresa, Christ is always a true friend at our side. This abiding sense of Christ's friendship was an enduring dimension of Teresa's spiritual journey.

A number of contemporary theologians writing from the perspective of women have pointed out that the Gospel accounts of the ministry of Jesus show that he modeled a way of relating that was characterized by friendship and mutuality rather than domination. This was evident in his own relationships with women and in the table fellowship he offered to people of many different backgrounds, including those who existed on the margins of the community. Reflecting on Jesus's liberating ministry, Elizabeth Johnson remarks, "New possibilities of relationships patterned according to the mutual services of friendship rather than domination-subordination flower among women and men who respond and join his circle."[4]

Characteristics of Friendship

Through the centuries theologians and spiritual writers have taught that reflecting on the characteristics of human friendship can help us to come to a better understanding of the dynamics of our relationship with Christ. Their writings invite us to consider the important friendships in our lives and to identify the "ingredients" in the recipe for a lasting friendship. Paul Wadell, a Catholic ethicist who has authored several works on friendship and the moral life, points out that classical authors set forth three distinguishing characteristics of friendship-love: benevolence, mutuality, and the capacity to look upon a friend as another self.[5] It is helpful, I believe, to explore these three characteristics and relate them to the invitation to friendship extended to each of us by the risen Christ.

First, *benevolence*. Benevolence means seeking the good of one's friend, of the beloved. A real friend wants what is truly best for us. And he or she desires that good not in some sort of detached, theoretical way, but in a very concrete, down-to-earth manner. A true friend is devoted to the well-being of the other. In his *Summa Theologiae*, Thomas Aquinas describes God's love for people as benevolence. God is always devoted to the well-being of God's beloved daughters and sons. God's love is totally other-centered; it is never for God's own "gain" in any way.

Second, *mutuality*. Sometimes we desire the good of another but do not experience that same desire in return. That can be a frustrating, even painful, experience. For genuine friendship to develop, there must be mutuality—reciprocity. Wadell says, "Friendship is mutual or reciprocal love in which each person knows that the good they offer another is also the good the other wishes for them. This second characteristic of friendship attests that friends are those that recognize each other's love and share it, the exchange of which is the soul of the relationship."[6] Real friendship is grounded in mutual concern, mutual gift.

This is precisely what we believe about the life of the Trinity, about what God is really like. Christians are convinced that God in Godself is a personal communion of life and love, an eternal dynamism of mutual giving and receiving. If we have been created in the image and likeness of God, we have been created in the image and likeness of the Trinity. That means we are "hardwired" for relationship. We are made for friendship.

Third, *seeing the friend as another self*. Classical thinkers tell us that this mutual sharing of love in friendship eventually leads each friend to see the other as "another self." This does not mean that we attempt to recreate our friends in our own image and likeness. It does not suggest that we see the friend as just an extension of ourselves, a kind of spiritual "clone." A true friend accepts the other for who he or she is. This characteristic means, rather, that through the love that binds friends together they become like one another in goodness and character.[7] There is a shared vision of life, especially of what is most important in life.

Benevolence, mutuality, the capacity to see the friend as another self: we can apply these three "friendship ingredients" to our relationship with Christ. First, benevolence, the strategy of devotion to the good of the other. This characteristic of friendship suggests that we need to learn to trust that Christ truly desires what is best for us. His strategy is devotion to our well-being. Sometimes it is difficult to recognize or feel that, especially in times of disappointment and suffering. In such periods, it can seem that Christ is far away from us, unresponsive to our pleadings. It is good to remember that Christ himself experienced this feeling of distance from his Father in his passion. The Gospels of Matthew and Mark describe him as praying the opening line of Psalm 22 from the cross: "My God, my God, why have you forsaken me?" (Matt 27:46; Mark 15:34). Nevertheless, he continued to hold onto the hand of God even at his darkest hour. And his resurrection from the dead showed that he was not, in reality, abandoned by the Father. We, then, are invited to renew our trust that the Lord Jesus is always present and on the move, seeking what is good for us, offering us life. Often that involves his capacity to bring life out of the "deathly" experiences of our lives. We need to become ever more convinced that Christ is not the detached, inaccessible Lord watching from afar to see how we will "score" on the tests of life. Rather, Christ is intimately involved in our lives and actively seeking our well-being.

How do we seek the well-being of Christ? How can we exercise benevolence toward Christ? It almost sounds odd to express it that way. But we can, in fact, exercise benevolence toward Christ by reflecting his presence and his love to others. By building up the Body of Christ. By attending to Christ in the people we encounter, especially those in need, as Pope Francis has reminded us again and again. There is a compelling expression of this idea in the writings of Gregory of Nazianzus, an important bishop and theologian of the fourth century. Gregory writes, "Let us visit Christ wherever we may; let us care for him, feed him, clothe him, welcome him, honor him....The Lord of all asks for mercy, not sacrifice, and mercy is greater than myriads of fattened lambs. Let us then show him mercy in the persons of the poor and those who today are laying on the ground, so that when we come to leave this world they may receive us into everlasting dwelling places."[8] Pope Francis echoes Gregory's sentiments in his exhortation on the call to holiness when he says that the best way to discern if our prayer is authentic is to judge to what extent our life is being transformed in the light of mercy (*Gaudete et Exsultate* 105).

What does mutuality in our relationship with Christ entail? It is important to realize that, when all is said and done, our life with God does not consist simply of completing a set of spiritual exercises, as if it were a spiritual "Olympic training." Spiritual exercises are essential, and we do need to cultivate self-discipline if our life with God is to flourish. But at its core, the life of the Spirit is an adventure of entrusting our lives and our very selves ever more fully to Christ and becoming ever more receptive to his gift of self to us. The heart of our life with God is personal self-gift, self-donation in response to God's self-communication in and through Christ. Fostering this mutuality requires us to accept Christ's love for us. Sometimes that is where we struggle the most; we draw back from the presence of Christ in anxiety or fear. We prefer to keep Christ at arm's length. We are acutely aware of our own weakness and sinfulness, and so we wonder why Christ would want to draw near to us. We may also be afraid of what Christ might ask of us. So it can be tempting to try to keep Christ at a safe distance. But if our friendship with Christ is to grow stronger, we must invite him to draw close to us and allow ourselves to receive from him. There is meant to be a true reciprocity in our friendship with Christ.

The capacity to see the friend as another self is reminiscent of a compelling, truly stunning, passage from Paul's Letter to the Galatians. The Apostle seems to lose himself as he reflects on the grace of God poured out in Christ: "I have been crucified with Christ; yet I live, no longer I, but Christ lives in me; insofar as I now live in the flesh, I live by faith in the Son of God who has loved me and given himself up for me" (Gal 2:19–20). Paul articulates his conviction that we discover our true selves in Christ. We become our best selves by staying connected to Christ, as the Gospel of John reminds us. Karl Rahner expressed this truth in a compelling way in his writings on theology and spirituality. In our ordinary experience, it is often the case that the more dependent we become on others, the less free, the less autonomous, we become. We speak of "codependence" to describe unhealthy relationships in which neither person is really free or able to mature as a person. But in our relationship with Christ *precisely the opposite* is the case. The more we come to depend on Christ—to root our entire lives in him—the freer, the more autonomous, the more "human" we become. This is true because we come to love the things that Christ loves. We learn to see life and other people more the way that Christ sees them. Through his grace, we become more like Christ in goodness and character.

Conclusion

So we begin by listening closely to the words of Jesus found in the Gospel of John: "I have called you friends." We are invited to allow those words to resound in our minds and hearts. We are summoned to recognize Christ as the one whose stance toward us is one of benevolence, the one who passionately desires to form a relationship of mutual love with us, and the one in and through whom we become our best selves.

FOR REFLECTION

- What do the traditional characteristics of friendship say to you about your relationship with Christ?
- Every friendship has its significant moments. What have been the significant moments in your friendship with Christ through the years?

Chapter 2

Christ the Healing Presence of God

We shift our focus now from the Gospel of John to the Gospel of Mark. In the first chapter of Mark's Gospel, we encounter Jesus as the proclaimer of the reign (kingdom) of God. The first words that Mark attributes to Jesus are, "This is the time of fulfillment. The kingdom of God is at hand. Repent, and believe in the gospel" (Mark 1:15). From that moment on in the Gospel, Jesus is on the move, proclaiming the reign of God in word and through his encounters with many kinds of people.

The Reign of God

The notion of the reign, or the kingdom, of God sounds mysterious to many people today. Some Christians immediately identify this "kingdom" with heaven, but the gospel references to the kingdom are more encompassing than that. This notion of God's kingdom has its roots in the Old Testament, for example, in psalms that celebrate God's reign over all of creation. In Psalm 96, the Psalmist evokes a sense of awe at God's rule:

Tremble before him, all the earth;

> declare among the nations: the LORD is king.
> The world will surely stand fast, never to be shaken.
> He rules the peoples with fairness. (Ps 96:9–10)

The prayers of ancient Israel make the bold claim that the God who had entered a covenant relationship with them was the God whose dominion extends throughout the entire universe. And through these prayers the people expressed their hope that God's reign would become manifest to all the nations.

The Gospels never depict Jesus sitting down with his disciples and giving them a "Webster's definition" of the reign of God. Rather, his descriptions are allusive; they are hinted at or implied in his provocative parables, his sayings about life in the kingdom, his table fellowship with both the powerful and the marginalized, and his healings and exorcisms. Jesus's announcement of the reign of God pointed to the longing of Israel for God to come in power and rule the world in the way that God had always intended. His proclamation evoked the dynamic notion of God powerfully ruling over God's people, indeed, over all of creation. The primary meaning of the reign of God, then, is dynamic, rather than spatial. It refers to an activity—God drawing near to establish God's rule in the world. Theologian Edward Schillebeeckx reflected deeply on the meaning of Jesus's proclamation of the reign of God. Schillebeeckx emphasized that Jesus's words about the kingdom reflect a God who is passionately concerned about humanity, whose coming rule means life and wholeness for people. The reign of God is "the saving presence of God, active and encouraging, as it is affirmed and welcomed among men and women."[1] Cardinal Walter Kasper, a theologian whose writings have inspired Pope Francis, describes the reign of God as "the sovereignty of God's love."[2] The kingdom comes, or it happens, when God's love is the ruling force in people's lives and relationships, indeed, within creation itself. The inbreaking of the kingdom entails the gracious drawing near of a loving God, whose very presence is transformative.

Jesus and the Leper

After recounting Jesus's initial announcement of the kingdom, Mark gives us a breathless account of the beginnings of his public ministry. On the initial "day" of his ministry, Jesus calls the first four disciples, frees a man tormented by an unclean spirit, cures Simon Peter's mother-in-law, and heals many others of the ill and possessed who crowd around the door of the house where he is staying. On the second "day," Jesus rises early and goes to a deserted place to spend time in prayer. Then Mark recounts an especially memorable encounter between Jesus and a man in desperate need:

> A leper came to him [and kneeling down] begged him and said, "If you wish, you can make me clean." Moved with pity, he stretched out his hand, touched him, and said to him, "I do will it. Be made clean." The leprosy left him immediately, and he was made clean. Then, warning him sternly, he dismissed him at once. Then he said to him, "See that you tell no one anything, but go, show yourself to the priest and offer for your cleansing what Moses prescribed; that will be proof for them." The man went away and began to publicize the whole matter. He spread the report abroad so that it was impossible for Jesus to enter a town openly. He remained outside in deserted places, and people kept coming to him from everywhere. (Mark 1:40–45)

The healing deeds of Jesus caused some people to wonder, to marvel at what had taken place and at the power of Jesus that was evident in the healing. Further along in the Gospel of Mark, when the restored Gerasene demoniac begins to proclaim what Jesus has done for him, Mark tells us that "all were amazed" (5:20). But the Gospels make it clear that this dimension of the marvelous was secondary to Jesus's real intent. Scripture scholar Donald Senior observes that the gospel miracle stories show that Jesus was a man of absolute integrity. His healing power never stepped outside the bounds of his mission, never betrayed the purpose of his ministry. Jesus never exploited his power for his own self-glorification.[3] These actions of healing were not intended as stupendous proofs of the coming of the kingdom; rather they were one of the means by which the kingdom came.[4] Jesus did not just talk about the reign of God; he made it present in the lives of the people he encountered. And when God's reign became present in and through Jesus, *people found life*. Women and men who had had the life drained out of them were enlivened and made whole.

Mark's story of the healing of the leper reflects this dynamic in a luminous way. This is a scene that is replete with divine power and raw human emotion. The leper is an outcast with a ravaged body and no future. This disease more than any other reminded biblical peoples of the power of death. Later rabbinic sayings compared a cure of leprosy to an act of raising someone from the dead.[5] The Book of Leviticus describes the stringent prescriptions of the Mosaic Law for people afflicted with leprosy, including the requirement that they take up residence "outside the camp" (Lev 13:45–46). This man has been compelled to exist on the peripheries of the community. The depth of his need is apparent in the way in which he approaches Jesus. First and foremost, he never should have come so close. He does so with apparent trust, but perhaps also out of sheer desperation. Mark places special emphasis on his action in approaching, using three participles in Greek: beseeching, falling to his knees, making a request. The direct manner in which he approaches Jesus suggests an implicit affirmation of Jesus's divine status, as does his bold statement, "If you wish, you can make me clean." This desperate man affirms Jesus's power to save.

Mark tells us that Jesus was "moved with pity" (1:41). This is a rather weak translation of a Greek term (*splagchnizomai*) that "designates the seat of affective feeling and emotion (our 'guts') and is often translated 'heart.'"[6] Jesus experiences a visceral reaction in this encounter; it is a gut-wrenching moment for him. The plight of this suffering man, an outcast from the community, moves him at the deepest part of his being. Jesus then does the unthinkable in reaching out to touch this leper, thereby incurring ritual defilement. Through his touch Jesus affirms his shared humanity with the leper and bridges the gap between the holy and the unclean.[7] For the people of Israel, life meant communion— communion with God and with one another. To be cut off from communion was to be as good as dead. By reaching out to touch this leper and healing him through his word, Jesus restores this man to communion. He raises him from spiritual death.

In scenes like this one, narrated so vividly by Mark, the evangelist wants his readers to know that the kingdom of God announced by Jesus is beginning to be present in his very ministry, even though the fullness of God's reign is yet to come. God is acting in a decisive way, drawing close to God's people. The forces that drain the life out of people are being confronted. People in need—those who have been deprived of life—experience restoration to life when they encounter this Jesus, who makes the gracious rule of God present. This is one of the gospel passages that undergirds Pope Francis's emphasis on *encounter* and his summons to Catholics to reach out to the existential peripheries. The leper, perhaps more than anyone, represented the existential periphery in Jesus's time and culture. And Mark's account portrays a liberating encounter between Jesus and this person on the margins.

A Modern Story of Healing

One of the most striking ways in which I have witnessed the healing power of Christ at work has been through retreats for persons in recovery from addictions. In listening to the stories of many of these women and men who have struggled with addiction, it has often struck me that they have felt like the "lepers" of our society. They have felt like outcasts whose addictions have led them into deadening isolation. So often people who are struggling with addiction experience a loss of communion with people they are closest to, with God, and even with themselves. But it is also very heartening to hear stories of recovery, where it becomes evident that the healing power of God in Christ is so very present and at work in the lives of these people. This is true even of those who do not use religious language in their accounts of their recovery.

I recall one woman, a member of a twelve-step recovery program, who participated in a weekend retreat at which I ministered. There was a large group of retreatants that weekend, some of them veterans of the program, while others were just off the streets and out of detox programs. It was a very down-to-earth crowd of folks. On the Friday evening of this retreat, I noticed a woman who appeared to be in her fifties. She had come to the retreat center from her job in a nearby city. I will call her Ruth. She was well-dressed, wearing a fashionable business suit. I soon discovered that she was originally from Ireland, and she had a lilting brogue to prove it. There was a sense of dignity and grace about Ruth. She had a kind, welcoming face and a gracious manner. I spoke with her briefly at meals and in the hallways during the weekend, though she was rather quiet in the large group gatherings that I attended.

The final session of the retreat on Sunday morning was a "gratitude sharing." It was an opportunity for anyone who wished to express their gratitude for the blessings of the retreat experience or, more generally, for the blessings they had received in their lives. Many women shared their reflections, some in quite dramatic fashion. Toward the end of this session, Ruth walked up to the podium and began to speak. She was modest and unassuming in her manner and choice of words, less dramatic than some of her fellow retreatants. But she was very well-spoken, and the room became quiet as the retreatants focused their attention on her words.

Ruth told the story of how she had come to the United States from Ireland in her twenties, accompanied by two friends. She had worked for a while as a nanny, but she lost that job because of her drinking. She then engaged in more menial forms of work but lost those jobs as well. Eventually, she found herself living on the city streets during a particularly harsh winter. She would spend the night at a woman's shelter and then return to the streets early in the morning, standing near the entrance of a subway stop as people arrived for their work. She was fortunate because one woman would give her a couple of dollars each day on her way to work. One of the social workers at the shelter took a special interest in her and convinced her to get help with recovery from her addiction. She also entered a job training program, eventually receiving the offer of an entry-level job at a large corporation. As of that retreat weekend, she had been working at that same corporation for more than twenty years, and now held a very responsible position. Looking at this woman as she related her story, I found it very hard to picture her homeless and begging at a subway stop. But that was what had happened in her life.

You could have heard a pin drop in that room as Ruth spoke of her gratitude to God for the ways in which God had brought healing to her life. She had come to a renewed sense of her Catholic faith through her journey from addiction to recovery, and it radiated from her. She spoke humbly, yet eloquently, of the healing and renewing power of God's grace. Ruth was a living reminder of grace, uttering her own modern-day version of the Magnificat. When I reflect on Jesus as the healing presence of God, I remember my encounter with Ruth.

Praying for Healing

It is difficult for some people to admit their need for the healing presence of Christ in their lives. We find it easier to pray for others in need of healing than to acknowledge the areas in our own lives that are wounded or broken and to bring them humbly to Christ. That kind of humble, honest prayer requires an openness and trust that can seem forbidding to us. It demands a stance of vulnerability that allows Christ to draw close to us. Sometimes we prefer to keep a "safe distance" from the Lord. Even in moments of great need, we can shield ourselves from the healing presence of Christ.

Some years ago, I experienced a number of significant losses in my life. I was the youngest of eight children, and my father had died when I was very young, leaving my mother to raise us. My mother died at the age of eighty-eight after suffering a stroke. Her final days were difficult for our family because she lingered for three weeks on the edge of death as we kept vigil. It was an excruciating time of waiting and accompaniment for us. A month after my mother died, one of my brothers, who was in his early sixties, died suddenly. During the following months, three close friends also died. I preached at four of those funerals and felt very drained at the end of those months.

Some months later, the effects of these losses began to make their impact on me. I found myself feeling very down, somewhat anxious, and struggling to meet my daily responsibilities. I soon realized that I needed to come before Christ and pray for healing and strength. In order to receive this healing, I had to battle my personal pride and ask for help in spiritual direction and some personal grief counseling. I like to think of myself as strong and not weak, but at that moment I was encountering my own weakness in a direct and quite humbling way. But I was blessed by the professional assistance of two fine people with whom I could talk and process the losses I had experienced. They became mediators of Christ's healing presence to me. Initially I found it very difficult to ask for help, though it was exactly the kind of help that I was used to recommending to other people who came to me in similar situations. Despite my pride and my initial reluctance, I realized how much I needed to seek that assistance. As a result, I experienced Christ's healing presence in my life in a whole new way.

It is important to step back periodically and ask ourselves if we are living in a healthy way. Am I cultivating good relationships with others, including solid friendships to which I am committed? Do I give those relationships the time and energy they deserve in order to grow and mature? Are there people in my life to whom I am close—family members, friends, and colleagues—who feel free to tell me when my thinking or behavior is becoming unhealthy, off-course? Do I listen to them, if they do tell me such a thing? Do I pursue a healthy balance in my life of work, leisure, prayer, and rest? Am I struggling with an addiction—to drugs, food, the Internet, work, or something else? What do I need to do to find help in recovering from that addiction? At this moment in my life, in what way do I need to experience the healing presence of Christ?

Every time we celebrate the Eucharist, we utter the words of the gospel centurion before receiving communion: "Lord, I am not worthy that you should enter under my roof, but only say the word and my soul shall be healed" (see Matt 8:8). Christ's gift of himself to us in the Eucharist is the primary way in which we experience his healing presence in our lives. His presence to us and with us restores our hope and empowers us to face the challenges in our lives. The sacrament of the anointing of the sick is another important means of receiving the Lord's healing. It is a gift that is not reserved for those who are dying but is available to all who stand in need of healing in a significant way. And, as in my own experience of loss, there are other ways of encountering the healing presence of God in Christ, and there are times in our lives when we need to make use of these other avenues of Christ's healing.

The Scars That Remain

I suspect that when some people think of the healing presence of Christ, they imagine that healing to be akin to "divine plastic surgery." They picture Christ as the preeminent plastic surgeon who is able to take their wounds, both the visible and invisible wounds, and so mend them that you would never even know they existed. Their wounds would be perfectly "smoothed over" with no remaining vestiges; there would be no scars.

But it does not usually happen in that way. Often the healing that Christ offers us, especially healing for the wounds that are most interior to us, entails the capacity to move on toward the future. The Lord empowers us to move ahead with freedom. His healing presence enables us not to stay stuck, mired in the negative and harmful dynamics of the past. The healing presence of Christ frees us from the specter of a past that compulsively crowds into and infringes upon our experience of the present, handicapping our ability to attend to the present. Usually, vestiges of the scars from the past remain and continue to creep into the present on occasion. Yet by continuing to bring those wounds before Christ, we do experience a deeper wholeness, and we are given the freedom to enter more fully into the present.

Pope Francis addressed this experience of wounds and the scars they leave in a retreat for priests that he gave in Rome in

2016. In his second meditation for that retreat, he referred to Jesus as the Father's mercy incarnate. He often speaks of Christ as the "face" of the Father's mercy. He proceeded to say that we can find the definitive icon of the vessel of mercy in the wounds of the risen Christ. Francis alludes to the wounds that we bear and the fact that they never completely disappear; they remain as scars. He cites two homilies of Bernard of Clairvaux, the Cistercian theologian and spiritual writer of the twelfth century, who invited his hearers to enter into the wounds of the Lord in order to discover mercy. Francis urged the priests on retreat to gaze at the wounds of the risen Christ, which remind us of our own wounds. He said, "God's mercy is in those scars, our scars." Referring to the Sacred Heart of Jesus, the pope said,

> As we contemplate the Lord's wounded heart, we see ourselves reflected in him. His heart and our own heart are similar: both are wounded and risen. But we know that his heart was pure love and was wounded because it willed to be so; our heart, on the other hand, was pure wound, which was healed because it allowed itself to be loved. By doing so, it became a vessel of mercy.[8]

One of my closest friends suffers from a form of mental illness caused by a chemical imbalance. Agnes (I will call her), with the aid of good psychiatric care and effective medication, functions at a high level. She is a person of deep faith who prays regularly. She often speaks of turning to Christ to ask for healing. Prayer is the constant source of her strength and consolation. The witness of faith that Agnes has given through the years has been a source of inspiration for me. Still, she wrestles with times of darkness marked by frustration, anxiety, and grief. Sometimes she asks, "Why do I have to suffer from this illness?" "Why doesn't my brain work right?" "Why did God allow this to happen to me?" Agnes and people like her sometimes find it difficult to read or hear gospel stories like that of the healing of the leper because they wonder why God does not offer them immediate healing, as Jesus did for the leper.

I am not able to offer any clinching answers to the questions that she raises in the dark times, especially the questions of the "why" of her illness. I wish that God would immediately "cleanse" her of her chemical imbalance in the same way that Jesus cleansed the leper of his dreaded disease. We cannot always understand the precise ways in which God responds to our prayers for healing. We can, however, be assured that through prayer we are given access to the *healing presence* of the crucified and risen Jesus. It is his merciful, loving presence that is the source of our deepest healing and our most enduring hope. It is the presence of a faithful, divine, and human companion who walks with us along the journey of our lives—the presence of the One who is risen with his wounds and whose scars are the source of our healing. As Pope Francis says, when we allow ourselves to be loved by the wounded Christ, we find healing, even when the scars remain.

We are invited, then, to approach the Lord Jesus, the healing presence of God in our world, with confidence. We can heed the invitation of Pope Francis to gaze on the wounds of the risen Christ and listen to his reminder that our hearts are healed by the heart of Christ when we allow ourselves to be loved by him. In a particular way, we are invited to bring to Christ the relationships in our lives that need his healing presence and touch. In our prayer, we can echo the words of the leper in the Gospel of Mark, "If you wish, you can make me clean." The gospel response of Jesus—"I do will it"—calls us to trust that he will respond to our prayer with his faithful, healing presence.

For Reflection

- Is there a Gospel story of healing that particularly resonates with you? What does it say to you?
- What areas of your life need the healing presence of Christ?

Chapter 3

Christ the Caller of Disciples

This Jesus whose presence brings hope and healing is the one who calls us to follow him on the road of discipleship. The gospel accounts of this dynamic of call portray Jesus acting in a way that was distinctive in comparison with other teachers of his day. Rather than the student seeking out the teacher and asking to be that teacher's disciple, Jesus initiated the call. He entered right into the midst of people's ordinary lives and invited them to embrace a radical reorientation of their pursuits and aims.

Turning to the Gospel of Matthew, we see Jesus call the fishermen Peter and Andrew as he walks along the Sea of Galilee. He summons them to follow him so that they can become fishers of men and women for the kingdom. Moving farther along the coastline, he calls the Zebedee brothers, James and John, to leave their father's boat and follow him. Later in the same Gospel, Jesus passes by Matthew's customs post and invites this despised tax collector to join the ranks of his disciples. As a result of that invitation, Jesus becomes the target of criticism from the religious leaders for associating with such people.

A gospel story that illumines the nature and dynamics of discipleship is Matthew's account of the calming of the sea. It is a passage that invites the reader to reflection and prayer:

> Then he [Jesus] made the disciples get into the boat and precede him to the other side, while he dismissed the crowds. After doing so, he went up on the mountain by himself to pray. When it was evening he was there alone. Meanwhile the boat, already a few miles offshore, was being tossed about by the waves, for the wind was against it. During the fourth watch of the night, he came toward them, walking on the sea. When the disciples saw him walking on the sea they were terrified. "It is a ghost," they said, and they cried out in fear. At once [Jesus] spoke to them, "Take courage, it is I; do not be afraid." Peter said to him in reply, "Lord, if it is you, command me to come to you on the water." He said, "Come." Peter got out of the boat and began to walk on the water toward Jesus. But when he saw how [strong] the wind was he became frightened; and, beginning to sink, he cried out, "Lord, save me!" Immediately Jesus stretched out his hand and caught him, and said to him, "O you of little faith, why did you doubt?" After they got into the boat, the wind died down. Those who were in the boat did him homage, saying, "Truly, you are the Son of God." (Matt 14:22–33)

It is intriguing that in the Gospels there is a noticeable undertone of humility that characterizes the portrayal of the disciples. It is not a triumphal picture of heroic strength. When we take a step back and think about that, we have to marvel. In the final third of the first century, the period in which most Scripture scholars think that the four Gospels were composed, Christians were a tiny minority of the population of the Roman empire. As such, they were vulnerable to misunderstanding and various forms of persecution. One might think that in their foundational documents they would have portrayed their leaders, those who were closest to Jesus, as unfailingly heroic, like some of the figures in Greco-Roman literature. The leading disciples were heroic in many ways, yet the Gospels also expose their weaknesses and tendency to failure. This is particularly true of the Gospel of Mark, in which the disciples seem to continue to misunderstand the teaching of Jesus, especially when he describes his own mission as one of service and giving his life for others (see Mark 10:45).

A similarly sober portrait of the disciples is found in the Gospel of Matthew, though not in quite as stark a manner as in Mark. Most scholars think that Matthew used the Gospel of Mark, as well as other sources, in composing his own Gospel. Passionist scripture scholar Donald Senior observes that in the Gospel of Matthew there is an unfinished quality to discipleship, one that precludes any sense of elitism or any confusion between master and teacher. There is only one master—Jesus the Messiah—and he remains the teacher of the ways of the reign of God. Disciples are always followers and learners.[1] One never "graduates" from discipleship and goes off on one's own. The disciple is always learning about the ways of God and is constantly called to follow along the way with Jesus.

This humility about discipleship in the Gospel of Matthew is evident in a characteristic Greek word that is distinctive to his Gospel; this term is translated into English as "you of little faith" (*oligopiste*; Matt 6:30; 8:26; 14:30–31; 16:8). There is a shift here from the Gospel of Mark, wherein the disciples are chided for their lack of faith, for having no understanding whatsoever (Mark 6:52; 8:21). In Matthew the disciples do have faith, but their faith is "little." The disciples do believe in Jesus, but they tend to be weak and hesitant in their faith.[2] They have a certain degree of insight into the identity and mission of Jesus, but they are prone to fear and anxiety. I believe that contemporary Christians can readily identify with the disciples in the Gospel of Matthew. Matthew's portrayal of discipleship and faith speaks to our experience.

The story of the calming of the sea and Peter's attempt to walk across the water is a classic instance of Matthew's description of the disciples. It is a particularly vivid account that is easy to picture in one's imagination. This gospel story has had special significance for me over the years. I have often been drawn to it in prayer, especially during times of turmoil and confusion. And I have frequently recommended this passage to other people for their prayer and reflection.

After Jesus has fed the five thousand, the disciples are crossing the lake at his command. He has told them to go on ahead of him to the other side of the lake, while he dismisses the crowds. Then he is rapt in prayer to the Father on a mountain. The disciples experience the ominous force of the sea; they are threatened by the powers of darkness, of the night. The winds are against them. They struggle long and hard against these terrifying forces until the fourth watch of the night, just before dawn. Amid this crisis, Jesus sees their struggle and comes to them. In the Gospels the boat can serve as a symbol for the church, the bark of Peter, and so the community for which Matthew wrote his Gospel would have been able to identify with this moment in the story. Scripture scholar John Meier comments on this scene beautifully: "In the church's direst need, when all seems lost, her Lord comes to save her, bestriding the waters of chaos."[3] Through his description of Jesus walking on the water, Matthew wants us to know that Jesus does what God does.

The disciples are panicked and cry out in fear. They are struggling for survival. But then the word of Jesus is addressed to them in the darkness of the night: "Take courage, it is I; do not be afraid." The words of Jesus, "It is I" (*ego eimi* in Greek), evoke the name of God in the Hebrew Scriptures. They echo the revelation of God's name to Moses near the burning bush (Exod

28

3:14–15). For the people of ancient Israel, the name of God was much more than an appellation; the divine name was a powerful reality that must be reverenced. It spoke to the people of Israel about the God who was present to save them and lead them into the future—the God who was with them and for them. The presence of God to Moses at the burning bush and the presence of God in and through Jesus amid the storm are not the incursions of some overpowering, numinous force from another world. It is a divine presence that is filled with intention, with God's passionate desire to reach out and to offer salvation to the people God loves. It is the presence and the word of Jesus that bring peace amidst the storm.

Then Peter springs into action. Peter, friend and companion of every disciple, utters his daring request: "Lord, if it is you, command me to come to you on the water." Peter is a disciple of contrasts in the Gospel of Matthew. This passage in chapter fourteen of the Gospel is the first in a series of texts that are distinctive in their focus on the person of Peter and his role of leadership among the disciples. In one of those texts, Peter will confess Jesus's identity as the Messiah and Son of God at Caesarea Philippi and receive the special blessing and designation as the "rock" on which Jesus will build his church (Matt 16:16–20). But Peter is also a very flawed disciple. In the story about the storm, we see both sides of Peter's character. He reflects both the strengths and weaknesses of Jesus's closest followers.

At first hearing, Peter's request to walk on the water sounds impulsive and presumptuous. In the Gospel of Matthew, however, the disciples are entrusted with the messianic powers of Jesus. Previously, in chapter ten of the Gospel, Jesus had given his disciples authority over unclean spirits and the power to cure every disease, as he commissioned them to go forth and proclaim the reign of God (Matt 10:1). The disciples are given a share in Jesus's power over the forces that oppress people and hold them in bondage. So in Matthew's narrative, Peter's request is not entirely presumptuous. Nevertheless, the special status of Peter and the authority he enjoys as a collaborator in Jesus's mission are tempered by Matthew's realistic assessment of his weakness. He fears the strength of the wind and begins to doubt the word of Jesus. He begins to sink into death.

As Peter becomes frightened and begins to sink, Jesus chides him for his "little faith." His faith is not absent, but it is "little." Meier points out that in the Gospel of Matthew the disciple is always someone who is caught between faith and doubt.[4] This doubt is not always theoretical. It can be practical doubt, that is, difficulty in acting on one's faith with courage. This ever-present tension is evident even in the majestic scene with which Matthew concludes his Gospel: the solemn commissioning of the disciples by the risen Jesus. Even at that moment in the story, Matthew tells us, "When they saw him, they worshiped, but they doubted" (Matt 28:17). So the situation of disciples being caught between faith and doubt continues even after the resurrection.

In the storm on the sea, then, Peter is emblematic of the disciples' struggle to believe in Jesus with a faith that is courageous, that does not hesitate when the forces of death are weighed against them. Even in his weakness and hesitancy, however, Peter is exemplary because he shows believers exactly what is needed in the midst of a crisis. He calls out, "Lord, save me!" Peter's cry for help echoes the prayer of the Psalmist in Psalm 69:

> Save me, God,
>> for the waters have reached my neck.
> I have sunk into the mire of the deep,
>> where there is no foothold. (Ps 69:2–3)

Here Peter shows us the way. This is exactly what the disciple of little faith must do. We must continue to cry out to the Lord in times of hesitation, doubt, or failure. In response, Jesus reaches out his hand, just as he has reached out his hand to heal the sick and possessed. Matthew tell us that Jesus does this "immediately"—without a moment's hesitation. Donald Senior observes that Jesus reaches out his hand "to rescue Peter from the terrifying abode of the deep and his paralyzing fear."[5]

This Gospel story concludes with a dramatic confession of faith on the part of the disciples: "Those who were in the boat did him homage, saying, 'Truly, you are the Son of God'" (Matt 14:33). This scene is an awe-inspiring revelation of the divine that evokes a proclamation of faith.

I believe that Christians today can find much in this passage that speaks to their lives. Yves Congar, a great twentieth-century Dominican theologian who played a key role at the Second Vatican Council, once gave a talk to priests from rural areas in France. He told those priests that when he spoke about matters of faith, he had to constantly apply to himself the words of the father who brought his son to Jesus's disciples for healing: "Lord, I believe, help my unbelief!" (see Mark 9:24). Congar reflected on the ways in which many modern people struggle with faith. He said, "But in the end everything is enclosed in faith."[6]

I find this Gospel depiction of disciples as people of little faith to be descriptive of my own experience of faith and discipleship. Ultimately, I do believe, and I cherish the gift of my faith. It is more important to me than anything. I like to tell myself that, as a vowed religious and priest, I have staked my life on the truth of my faith. Yet when I am honest with myself, I know that my faith is often weak and hesitant, like that of the disciples in the Gospel of Matthew. Faith can seem so fragile at times. When the winds are sweeping across the waters and rocking the boat, I often find it difficult to show boldness in faith. I can readily identify with the flawed and ambivalent disciples in the Gospel. Admitting those struggles with faith is humbling but also realistic, and it is the only way for our faith to grow and mature.

Faith in the Contemporary World

In reflecting on the meaning and the dynamics of faith, I have found the insights of Jesuit theologian Gerald O'Collins to be illuminating. O'Collins appeals to three "C's" in his discussion of faith.[7] His schematic helps us to unpack and reflect on faith — what it is and how it is expressed in our lives. O'Collins speaks of faith as *confession, commitment,* and *confidence.* All three of these dimensions of faith are integral to the life of the Christian disciple. By *confession* O'Collins is referring to the cognitive content of faith, to the truths about God's self-revelation to which we assent. These truths (doctrines) mediate the reality of God's self-revelation in history. Each Sunday we stand and profess the Creed at the Eucharist. This is a liturgical expression of our assent to the central truths of our faith about God's self-communication through Jesus and in the Holy Spirit. We believe that God has given of Self in an unsurpassable way in Jesus; God has given of Self as One to be known and loved. Faith as *confession* pertains to the *past* dimension of the virtue of faith. It refers to the saving deeds of God in history, witnessed to by the people of ancient Israel and the apostles, and expressed in the Tradition that has been handed down to us.

Followers of Jesus instinctively know, however, that confession of the truths of faith is not complete without personal *commitment.* If *confession* is related to God's self-revelatory and salvific deeds of the past, *commitment* pertains to the *present* dimension of faith. It entails our personal surrender to the God whom we encounter in the person and deeds of Jesus Christ. It means entrusting myself and my life to God, something not accomplished in a single act, of course, but which must be renewed again and again in new times and circumstances. As we saw in the first chapter, this is the God who in Jesus has called us to live in friendship, in a life-giving relationship of mutual love.

Confidence refers to the *future* dimension of faith. It pertains to that for which we hope. Confidence entails trust in God's promises to us. It means that we grow in our trust that God is faithful to us, that ultimately God keeps God's promises. This is the deep trust that the Gospel of Luke attributes to Mary in the Magnificat:

> He has helped Israel his servant,
> remembering his mercy,
> according to his promise to our [ancestors],
> to Abraham and to his descendants forever.
>   (Luke 1:54–55)

It is this confidence that gives rise to boldness in faith. It enables us to move from "little faith" to strong, mature faith.

Confession, commitment, confidence—three essential dimensions of the one virtue of faith. Most of us do relatively well with the confessional dimension of faith. There is a pluralism of theologies in the contemporary church, especially with the burgeoning of diverse cultural perspectives on the gospel. These distinct cultural expressions give witness to the richness of God's self-revelation. Sometimes there is disagreement over the interpretation of doctrine. But most Catholics adhere to the heart of the Christian faith as it is mediated to us by Scripture and Tradition.

I suspect that it is in the commitment and confidence dimensions that we often find ourselves to be disciples of "little faith." We are committed to Christ by our baptism, and we renew that commitment in the celebration of the Eucharist as well as in other sacramental encounters and in moments of personal prayer. But that commitment, as much as we want it to be wholehearted, remains something incomplete for most of us. There are aspects of our lives that we try to safeguard and keep away from Christ. We tend to compartmentalize our lives. Our personal surrender to Christ is less than complete. The ancient fathers and mothers of the desert understood their lives to be an ongoing quest for purity of heart, which meant wholehearted commitment to Christ. That is our search, too, as we strive to allow Christ to break into our lives and to shape our desires, affections, and choices. In *Lumen Fidei*, the encyclical begun by Pope Benedict XVI and completed by Pope Francis, the popes said, "We believe in Jesus when we personally welcome him into our lives and journey towards him, clinging to him and following his footsteps along the way" (no. 18). This is a compelling expression of the commitment dimension of faith—personally welcoming Jesus into our lives over and over again, journeying toward him, clinging to him.

Confidence. Sometimes the disappointments of life and the disillusionment they cause can weaken or even undermine our confidence. Everyone is at one time or the other in their lives confronted with broken promises. The experience of promises not kept can make it difficult to trust that anyone is really faithful to their promises, even God. When we meet a person who is filled with cynicism, we can be fairly sure that at some point in that person's life some important promises were broken. As we grow in our relationship with Christ, we are challenged to deepen our confidence that the future rests in the hands of a faithful God. We are invited to renew our trust that God really does keep God's promises to us—promises to offer us new life over and over again. We are invited to reaffirm our trust that when we, like Peter, are sinking into the sea of chaos, Christ will stretch out his hand to save us, and he will do that immediately. In a letter that Pope Francis addressed to consecrated women and men, he commented, "None of us should be dour, discontented and dissatisfied, for a 'gloomy disciple is a disciple of gloom.' Like everyone else, we have our troubles, our dark nights of the soul, our disappointments and infirmities, our experience of slowing down and growing older. But in all these things we should be able to discover 'perfect joy.'" Pope Francis gives us a tall order, but I believe that his words about Christian joy apply not only to consecrated men and women but to all disciples. Internalizing this joy is possible only if we renew the confidence dimension of our faith time and time again. We are invited to believe that God keeps God's promises, in fact, that God is tenaciously faithful to us. My very wise novice director, Father Raphael Amrhein, used to counsel his novices, "Don't deny in the darkness what you have seen in the light." What has been revealed in the light given by Christ is the God who is faithful to God's promises.

Witnesses of Faith

When I reflect on this theme of discipleship and faith, I am reminded of encounters I have had over the years with Catholics from China—laypersons, vowed religious, and priests. I have been privileged to teach a number of Chinese students in two different schools of theology and ministry. Many of these students have intriguing stories of faith. Some have endured significant hardship because of the practice of their faith, especially if they have decided to study overseas for ministry. Catholics and other Christians in China often must negotiate formidable obstacles in order to practice their faith, and sometimes they put themselves and their families in danger by doing so.

Several members of my own Passionist community served in the Hunan province of China from the 1920s into the 1950s. Father Marcellus White was one of those missionaries. He served as a priest in China until he was expelled from the country after the Communist regime rose to power. Marcellus went to China in 1935 and energetically served as a priest for fifteen years. When the Communist leaders assumed power and spread their influence throughout China, he was suspected of being a spy because he had served as a United States Air Force chaplain. He was initially placed under house arrest in 1951 and then imprisoned in 1953, where he was kept in solitary confinement. Sometimes he was compelled to request permission from the guards simply to stand up, sit down, or lie down. He was expelled from the country in 1955 and in 1958 went to the Philippines, where he ministered as a missionary for more than thirty years. In later years, after China became open to the West, Marcellus traveled back to China and met some of the people to whom he had ministered as a priest forty years earlier. During one of those trips, officials at a Communist Party museum showed Marcellus a photo of himself, which honored his assistance to the people of China during World War II. I once invited Marcellus to visit some students from China at the school of theology where I was teaching. He was overjoyed to meet these students and to speak Chinese with them. He loved the people of China and wanted to know as much as possible about the state of the church there.

Marcellus occasionally spoke about his experience of imprisonment in China. He once mentioned that his best years as a Passionist priest were when he was there in prison, in solitary confinement. When I first heard that, it sounded to me like a bit of "missionary hyperbole." But the longer I knew Marcellus, the truer his words seemed to me. It was there in solitary confinement that he realized most keenly his absolute dependence on God. He had nothing and no one but Christ to hold onto in that dark night of faith deep in the heart of China. Like Peter trying to walk on the windswept sea in the dark of night, Marcellus realized that all he could do was to cry out, "Lord, save me." He had to grasp onto the outstretched hand of Christ. As terrible as those days must have been, Marcellus gained a deep appreciation of them later in his life.

Most of us will never experience the persecution and hardship that Marcellus encountered as a missionary. Today, however, many thinkers observe that in an increasingly secularized world, it takes great courage to live as a person of faith. No longer is it assumed that people will practice religious faith. Faith in God, or in a transcendent Power, is now just one option among many others for a way to find meaning in one's life. Karl Rahner addressed this reality more than forty years ago in an essay about the spirituality of the future. He observed that, at least in Western society, the social supports for religious faith had crumbled and thus the responsibility of making a decision of faith rested with the individual. Rahner concluded, "That is why the modern spirituality of the Christian involves courage for solitary decision contrary to public opinion, the lonely courage analogous to that of the martyrs of the first century of Christianity, the courage for a spiritual decision of faith."[8] Rahner went on to assert that the Christian of the future will be a mystic or he or she will not exist at all. By "mystical" Rahner was referring not to extraordinary parapsychological phenomena, but to "a genuine experience of God emerging from the very heart of our existence."[9] Today a vital Christian life requires a courageous response of faith to the personal call of Jesus to follow him on the road of discipleship. It grows out of an encounter with God in Christ Jesus. And it entails faith in all its dimensions—confession, commitment, and confidence.

So we are invited to come before the Lord Jesus honestly with our "little faith." In that encounter we can express our gratitude for the gift of faith, which is the pearl of great price in our lives. We can also bring the doubts with which we struggle directly to Christ. There we can pray for the grace to be strengthened in our personal commitment to him and in our confidence in his fidelity to us. And we are invited to listen as Christ comes to us across the water and says, "Take courage, it is I; do not be afraid."

FOR REFLECTION

- Read Matthew 14:22–33. Imagine yourself with the disciples in the boat, tossed about by the waves. Accompany Peter as he attempts to walk on the water toward Jesus. Feel the strength of the wind. Envision Jesus stretching out his hand to rescue you from drowning.

- In your prayer, express your gratitude to God for the gift of faith. Bring any doubts you are struggling with honestly and directly to Christ. Ask the Lord to strengthen your commitment to him and to increase your confidence in his presence in your life.

Chapter 4

Christ the Bread of Life

Human beings are very hungry creatures. Our hungers—our desires—are intensely powerful forces in our lives. And what we crave can come to rule our thinking and our behavior. Sometimes we are not even aware of the deep desires that are compelling us to think and act the way we do.

I caught a glimpse of the power of hunger during a trip to Haiti two years after the 2010 earthquake there, which tragically killed hundreds of thousands of people and devastated much of the country. I traveled to Haiti to visit a fellow Passionist, Rick Frechette. Frechette is a priest and a physician who, along with his Haitian colleagues and volunteers from many countries, has taken the lead in building hospitals, orphanages, schools, and housing projects that serve the needs of very impoverished people. After the 2010 earthquake, Frechette and his associates devoted special attention to those whose lives were most adversely affected by it, including the many people who were forced to live in tent cities and others who resided in dangerous housing conditions. They also had to confront the cholera epidemic that spread in the wake of the earthquake—a terrible one-two punch that exacerbated the suffering of the people.

There is a group in the organization founded by Frechette that produces large bags of precooked pasta. When the refugees from the earthquake were living in the tent cities, some of these workers regularly delivered bags of pasta to them. On one day during my visit, I accompanied five of these workers on one of their deliveries. We rode in a small flatbed truck, with three of us sitting in the front of the truck and three standing among the bags of pasta in the back. The food distribution was usually organized through local leaders, who would give out tickets to the neediest people in the area, beginning with the elderly and mothers of small children. For this delivery we drove to Cité du Soleil, one of the most impoverished and underserved localities in the Western Hemisphere. When we arrived that day, however, the local leader was inexplicably absent, and the distribution system broke down. So the truck was surrounded by a large crowd of people in great need, each of whom wanted a bag of pasta. The workers labored intensely to distribute the food in the most orderly and fair manner that they could. But the scene soon became tense, even a little chaotic. Eventually, they finished distributing all the bags of pasta that we had brought with us and we drove away, leaving some very disappointed and frustrated people behind. Frechette and his colleagues had to arrange for another delivery in that area and assure that the local leader would be present to monitor it.

As we drove off in the truck that day, I could not help but reflect on the power of hunger in our lives. The people whom we met in Cité du Soleil had been tragically displaced by an earthquake, forced to exist in tents for more than two years after that devastating disaster. Hunger must have become an ever-present reality for many of them as they scraped to make a living any way they could. Their hunger was—very understandably—a powerful driving force in them. I could feel the force of that hunger as I helped to distribute the bags of pasta. It was personally very difficult to sit in that truck as we drove away that day, leaving many unsatisfied people behind. I could only trust that these deliveries would continue and that dedicated people like Father Frechette would continue to reach out generously to these people in such great need. I had been aware of the facts of hunger in the world, but feeling the force of it while sitting in that truck was quite another thing.

Getting in Touch with Our Hungers

In my ministry as a Passionist priest I have witnessed the powerful force of hunger in the people I have served. That has included physical hunger among the homeless, the hunger for love and attention that marks the lives of many young people, the yearning for companionship seen in the faces of elderly women and men who traverse the corridors of nursing homes, and hunger in its many other forms. Pastoral ministers can often perceive the deep-seated, potent hungers that drive people in ways of which they are often not even conscious. Sometimes these cravings impel them to pursue good, worthwhile accomplishments, while at other times they lead them in directions that are deceptive or even destructive.

All of us are to some extent driven by more superficial cravings. These include the desire to accumulate more and better possessions, a desire that is fed by the consumerist society in which we live. The innumerable advertisements that bombard us on television and through email and social media can be difficult to ignore. And there are so many other passions that compel us: the search for distraction and pleasure, where life can become all about entertainment; the quest for popularity and recognition by our peers; the passion for prestige in the communities in which we live; the craving for attention from family members and friends.

If we are at all self-reflective, we also come into touch with our deeper, more transcendent hungers: the desire to be loved and affirmed by significant people in our lives; our need for faithful friendship; the yearning to make a genuine contribution to the world, to have a sense that our lives have made a real difference to others; our hope that the bonds of faith and love that we have forged throughout our lives will not be severed by death; and ultimately our deep-seated desire to see the face of God and live. Often it is in the hard times, the times of loss or other personal suffering, that we touch these deeper desires in ourselves and in those we love and serve. The experience of loss has a way of shining a light on what is most important in life. These more profound desires are the points of connection for the experience of grace—God's self-communication to us. They are the places where the presence and action of God light up in our lives.

If we are committed Christians—whether lay, vowed religious, or ordained—that deep passion for God in our hearts has led us to respond to Jesus's invitation to discipleship. We have been impelled to follow Jesus by the vivifying action of the Holy Spirit, who awakens and enlivens our hunger for God. But there are times in the journey of discipleship when we lose touch with our desire for God, and the flame of faith within begins to smolder. The frustrations and disappointments of life can dampen that passion. We need to reawaken and to nourish that deep desire for the God who, as Saint Augustine came to see, has given us restless hearts that will not find true rest until they rest in God. Those who can nourish that passion for God remain vital in the life of Christian discipleship. They mature in their faith and become living sacraments of Christ's presence for others.

Nourished by the Eucharist

The Second Vatican Council (1962–65) taught that the Eucharist is both the source and the summit of the Christian life. It is the source from which we find the nourishment, energy, and courage we need to follow the Lord Jesus. Celebrating the

Eucharist nourishes and inflames our passion for God. And the celebration of the Eucharist is the summit, the highest expression, of our lives as Christians. It contains and signifies the heart of our life as disciples of Jesus.

In a pastoral letter addressed to the Archdiocese of Chicago, the late Cardinal Joseph Bernardin observed that it is in the Eucharist that we discover *who* we are and *whose* we are. In the celebration of this sacrament, we discover our true identity as disciples of Jesus and daughters and sons of God. We celebrate the Eucharist regularly in order to mature in our consciousness of our essential identity. Our identity—who we are—is inextricably linked with our belonging to God in Christ. We are called to approach our lives out of the awareness that in Christ we belong to God; we are God's own. Amidst the daily routines and the challenges of everyday life, it is easy to lose sight of that God-given identity and to lose sight of the One to whom we belong. We need to keep returning to the table of the Word and Sacrament to awaken that awareness. We need to keep telling the story of God's gracious, lavish love poured out in Jesus Christ. And we need to continue to open our minds and hearts to receive Christ's gift of himself to us in the Eucharist.

The Eucharist is akin to an exquisite diamond with many facets. No single author or book can exhaust the meaning of this sacrament. In this reflection I wish simply to focus on the Eucharist as food for the journey of discipleship. Through the gift of the Eucharist, God elicits and nourishes the deepest human hungers that lie within us. God satisfies the hungry human heart with the gift of finest wheat.

In the Bread of Life discourse from the sixth chapter of the Gospel of John, we find these words:

> [Jesus said]: "I am the living bread that came down from heaven; whoever eats this bread will live forever; and the bread that I will give is my flesh for the life

of the world." The Jews quarreled among themselves, saying, "How can this man give us [his] flesh to eat?" Jesus said to them, "Amen, amen, I say to you, unless you eat the flesh of the Son of Man and drink his blood, you do not have life within you. Whoever eats my flesh and drinks my blood has eternal life, and I will raise him on the last day. For my flesh is true food, and my blood is true drink. Whoever eats my flesh and drinks my blood remains in me and I in him. Just as the living Father sent me and I have life because of the Father, so also the one who feeds on me will have life because of me. This is the bread that came down from heaven. Unlike your ancestors who ate and still died, whoever eats this bread will live forever." (John 6:51–59)

This rich gospel text invites us to sustained reflection. It is found near the end of the sixth chapter of the Gospel of John. Prior to this discourse, Jesus has provided nourishment to the crowd of five thousand who had followed him across the Sea of Galilee. He took the loaves and fish, gave thanks, and distributed them to the crowds. The next scene is John's account of Jesus walking on the water and encountering the disciples, who are in a boat that is being rocked by a strong wind. The words he speaks to them are familiar: "It is I. Do not be afraid." It is then that Jesus engages in a lengthy dialogue with the crowds and the religious leaders, who have come back across the Sea of Galilee to Capernaum, looking for him. As is true throughout the Gospel of John, the conversation has distinct levels of meaning. The crowds have just been fed with physical food through the multiplication of the loaves and fish. Jesus questions their motives for returning to him, concluding that they are seeking him only because they have eaten their fill: "Amen, amen, I say to you, you are looking for me not because you saw signs but because you ate the loaves and were filled. Do not work for food that perishes but for the food that endures for eternal life, which the Son of Man will give you" (John 6:26–27). Jesus invites them to discover in him the one who can satisfy their deepest human longings.

The crowds, however, recall Moses feeding their ancestors in the desert with manna. Jesus challenges them again, reminding them that it was not Moses who fed the people but his Father in heaven. When the people ask Jesus to give them the "bread of God" that comes from heaven, Jesus identifies himself with this food: he is the Bread of Life. And the conversation continues, with some in the crowd questioning Jesus for making such an extraordinary claim. How can Jesus be the true bread from heaven when they know where he comes from? They know his parents, his earthly origins. The question of Jesus's true origins is a pivotal one in the Gospel of John. In the trial scene of John's passion narrative, Pilate will ask Jesus, "Where are you from?" (John 19:9). For the author of this Gospel, that is exactly the right question to ask—the question of Jesus's true origins. But Pilate never grasps the true answer to his question, and neither do many others in the Gospel narrative. They cannot seem to perceive that Jesus's real origins are in God.

In the section of the Bread of Life discourse quoted above, the eucharistic overtones sound forth clearly. New Testament scholars observe that the eucharistic tradition of the Johannine community lies in the background of the Gospel narrative. The community that gave birth to this Gospel and the three letters of John had a rich but troubled history. It appears that it was embroiled in tensions within the community and conflicts with others who did not share their faith in Jesus. If there was any community in the early church that needed the unifying effects of the Eucharist, it was the Johannine community. The Gospel writer was reminding the believers for whom he was writing that they encounter Christ, the true Bread of Life, through their sharing in the Eucharist.

We find the word *remain* in this passage: "Whoever eats my flesh and drinks my blood remains in me and I in him" (John

6:56). We encountered this important Johannine term in the first chapter of this book, in the context of the discourse on the vine and the branches. Followers of Jesus are invited to remain—or abide—in Jesus in order to find the strength, nourishment, and direction they need in their lives. To have eternal life, about which this Gospel often speaks, means to live in close communion with Jesus—to live connected to him. Jesus is not simply a memorable figure of the distant past. He is a living person, who invites us into a vital relationship with him. Nowhere is this abiding in Jesus, this communion with Jesus, more real than in the celebration of the Eucharist.

The terms that Jesus employs in the Bread of Life discourse are remarkably concrete, even earthy. Scripture scholars underline the earthy quality of the words ascribed to Jesus: "Unless you eat the flesh of the Son of Man and drink his blood, you do not have life within you" (John 6:53). The Greek words that are employed by the author are unusually graphic. This graphic, down-to-earth language points us to the stark reality of the death of Jesus, his literal laying down of his life for all people: "The bread that I will give is my flesh for the life of the world" (John 6:51). Jesus will become the source of life for all people, the true Bread of Life, through his complete gift of himself for the life of the world. This self-gift will be offered through his entering into the darkness of a violent death. It will be an exceedingly earthy and pain-filled act. Jesus will nourish the entire world with the gift of himself.[1] This means that remaining in Jesus, abiding in him, entails the willingness of those who celebrate and receive the Eucharist to lay down their lives for others. Disciples are called to emulate the One who nourishes others with the gift of himself. We are called to make our lives eucharistic.

Whenever I read the Bread of Life discourse in the Gospel of John, I am reminded of the Academy Award winning film *Life Is Beautiful*. Starring Roberto Benigni, this touching film tells the story of a young Jewish family living in Italy during World War II.

Benigni's character is that of a zany, bumbling Italian waiter living in a small town who falls madly in love with the schoolteacher in the town. They are married and give birth to a son. He is very devoted to his wife, and both take great delight in their son. But the three of them are rounded up and deported by train to a concentration camp, along with many of their fellow Jews. In its story, the movie subtly interweaves the exquisite beauty of devoted love with the insidious power of evil.

The movie depicts the way in which the life of the prisoners is slowly, systematically drained out of them in the concentration camp. But amid this enveloping darkness, the young father, now separated from his wife, does everything in his power to save his son. He is ingenious in devising ways to give life to his son and to keep the menacing power of evil from destroying the boy. He convinces his son that the entire scenario is really a game in which they must accumulate points to win the grand prize. The father is comical whenever he can be to keep his son from succumbing to the grayness and unrelenting hardship in the camp. His is a love that is clever and creative in discovering ways to shield and spare his beloved child. It is a love that entails extraordinary sacrifice, the offering of his very life to the very end.

There is one scene in *Life Is Beautiful* that particularly reminds me of the gift of the Eucharist. It is quite far-fetched historically, but it is very effective in the narrative of the movie. It is the scene of a festive dinner given in the camp for the German officers and their families. A German physician whom the father had known before the war recommends him for service as the waiter for the dinner. The father is hoping against hope that this doctor will intervene to save him and his son. As the father diligently waits on the tables filled with Nazi officers and their wives, his son sits silently in an adjoining room with the children of the military officers. No one knows that the boy is a Jew. This festive, life-giving meal is a momentary reprieve from the experience of deprivation and degradation in the camp. And the father joyfully

47

serves the delicious food to his beloved son, who sits among the other children. The father, who loves his son so intently and is working so tirelessly to save him, delights in nourishing him with the food from the banquet.

This poignant scene from *Life Is Beautiful* speaks to me about Christ the Bread of Life. It offers a little glimpse of what Christ does for us every time we come to the Eucharist. And it brings together in a compelling way the elements of sacrifice and meal, cross and table, that are essential to the full meaning of the Eucharist. This Jesus who gave his life on the cross for the world, who spoke of giving his flesh for the life of the world, delights in giving his life to us in the Eucharist. He labors tirelessly to nourish us with the bread of life, which he in fact is. And he takes great delight when we come to him to receive the nourishment we need for the journey of discipleship.

Nourished throughout Our Lives

The risen, living Jesus has his own inventive, often mysterious, ways of nourishing us along the journey of discipleship. When I was a college seminarian, I took several courses in theology from a professor who was a Dominican priest and who later went on to teach in Africa. He was a learned scholar and a very effective teacher. But in addition to his intellectual acumen and pedagogical skills, he also had a wisdom that was deeper than mere intelligence. I sometimes visited this professor to seek his guidance in the discernment of my vocation.

I vividly remember one conversation with him in particular. I had become very discouraged about considering a call to religious life and priesthood. Some of the interactions I had experienced in the local formation community had been disappointing for me. And I was growing doubtful about my own ability to serve as a Passionist priest. I was beginning to think that I did not "have what it takes." So I spoke at some length about these doubts with this priest-professor. He listened very attentively to my angst-filled discourse. When I finally finished speaking, the two of us just sat in silence for a few moments. And then he said to me, "Robin, you just have to learn to trust that Jesus always gives us what we need."

I was surprised and rather perplexed by his response. After all, this was a learned professor of theology and an experienced spiritual guide. I was expecting a response that was more subtle and sophisticated than the one that he gave me. At first, his words sounded simplistic to me. They reminded me of a "bumper sticker" platitude that one might see on the back of a car. I did not quite know how to respond to him. In the days following our conversation, however, his words kept coming back to my mind. I began to ponder what they might mean for my life.

I have often recalled the words of this priest-professor in the many years since that day. The response that he gave me has come back to me in moments of struggle and need in my own life. I have said to myself on many occasions, "Robin, in this situation, too, you have to learn to trust that Jesus always gives us what we need." Through the years, I have discovered the truth of those words. This certainly does not mean that Christ miraculously preserves us from every situation of disappointment, loss, struggle, or pain. It does not mean that we do not come face-to-face with our own weakness and inadequacies at times. It does not mean that we never feel hungry or unsatisfied by life. Sometimes we suffer from a gnawing hunger for companionship, personal support, and meaning.

The truth that my professor spoke to me does mean that despite the way we may feel at times, we are never alone on the journey of discipleship. Christ walks with us in every situation of our lives, the joyful and satisfying experiences as well as the painful and wrenching ones. He is in radical solidarity with us. He invites us to grasp onto his hand for the strength we need to face the challenges that are before us. And Christ is ingenious in finding ways to nourish us, not only in the sacraments but also through the people he places in our lives. He continues to give us what we need, sometimes in ways and through people that we least expect.

So we are invited to gaze on the face of Christ, the Bread of Life. And we are called to heed the words of the Gospel of John to "remain" in him—to abide in Christ through our faithful participation in the Eucharist as well as by living in his presence in all the endeavors of ordinary life. We are called to hold onto the hand of Christ, who accompanies us and continues to nourish us on our journey as his disciples. He continues to offer us the Bread of Life—the gift of himself, which satisfies the hungry heart.

FOR REFLECTION

- What does the gift of the Eucharist mean to you? What role does it play in your life with God?
- How have you experienced Christ giving you what you needed at moments of difficulty and struggle in your life?

Chapter 5

Christ the Good Shepherd

We turn now to gaze on the face of Jesus Christ who is the Good Shepherd. This image of Christ is a familiar one, featured prominently in the tenth chapter of the Gospel of John and celebrated by Christians when we pray the cherished Twenty-Third Psalm. Jesus himself describes his Father as a shepherd whose care for the sheep is so faithful that he goes in search of the one sheep that has become lost, separated from the rest of the fold (Luke 15:1–7). In this reflection on Christ as the Good Shepherd, I am going to focus on the reconciling work of Christ. Christ is the shepherd who reconciles us with God and with one another.

The Reconciling Ministry of Christ

In the Second Letter to the Corinthians, Paul reflects on his own ministry as an apostle in light of God's reconciling action in Christ. He envisions his apostolic ministry as propelled by the love of Christ, as he writes, "For the love of Christ impels us, once we have come to the conviction that one died for all" (2 Cor

5:14). Christ's redemptive love makes those who are "in Christ" a new creation: "Behold, new things have come" (2 Cor 5:17). At the origin of this entire dynamic of reconciliation is God: "God was reconciling the world to himself in Christ, not counting their trespasses against them and entrusting to us the message of reconciliation" (2 Cor 5:19).

Paul's articulation of the saving work of God in Christ is especially important for Christian theology and spirituality. It assures us that the entire Christ-event—the life, ministry, death, and resurrection of Jesus—was the *result* of God's salvific love for the human family. It is *not* the case that the death of Jesus appeased the wrath of an "angry God" who was ready to condemn us. Sadly, this has sometimes been the picture of redemption that has been presented in Christian theology and preaching. Rather, it was God's passionate desire to offer salvation to humanity—to reconcile us to Godself—that was the source of everything that Jesus said and did. Christ was God's embrace of a wounded world. In and through Christ, God was reaching out to reconnect to Godself human beings who had disconnected themselves from God and from one another through sin. Paul names and celebrates the reconciling love of God in Christ, and he envisions his own apostolic ministry as an extension of this divine work of reconciliation in history. He has been called to be an "ambassador" of Christ the Reconciler: "So we are ambassadors for Christ, as if God were appealing through us. We implore you on behalf of Christ, be reconciled to God" (2 Cor 5:20). Paul is convinced that he must spend his life proclaiming and making present the reconciling work of God in Christ.

The Primacy of Mercy

Christian discipleship, then, includes the call to live as *reconciled* and *reconciling* people. And this vocation to serve as ambassadors of reconciliation for Christ is grounded in the experience of God's gracious mercy. It is because we have encountered the mercy and compassion of God in our own lives that we are enabled to be agents of reconciliation in the world. Therefore, our call to live as reconciled and reconciling people is a response to grace. The Carmelite poet Jessica Powers (1905–88), known in religious life as Sister Miriam of the Holy Spirit, expressed this truth beautifully in a poem titled "The Mercy of God."[1] She speaks of the day on which she ceased to fear God "with a shadowy fear." It happened not because she realized how virtuous she had become but because, "I began to see truly that I came forth from nothing and ever toward nothingness tend." Powers depicts this spiritual awakening as a walk into the woods: "I rose up from the acres of self that I tended with passion and defended with flurries of pride; I walked out of myself and went into the woods of God's mercy, and here I abide." In these "woods," Powers finds "greenness and calmness and coolness." This movement out of self into the "woods of God's mercy" is what liberated her from a "shadowy" fear of God: "And I fear God no more; I go forward to wander forever in a wilderness made of His infinite mercy alone." Commenting on Powers's poem, Robert Morneau observes, "It is the experience of God's infinite mercy that brings peace and greenness and calmness and coolness."[2]

Pope Francis has consistently highlighted the primacy of divine mercy in his preaching and writing. He dedicated an Extraordinary Jubilee Year to the theme of divine mercy. Francis envisages Christian life with God as first and foremost a *response to grace*. He often cites a passage from the First Letter of John: "In this way the love of God was revealed to us: God sent his only Son into the world so that we might have life through him. In this is love: not that we have loved God, but that he loved us and sent his Son as expiation for our sins. Beloved, if God so loved us, we also must love one another" (1 John 4:9–11). God's grace always goes first. Our task is to respond to that grace. Francis detects vestiges of the fifth-century heresy of Pelagianism that he thinks are still evident in the lives of Christians, that is, a view that minimizes the importance of God's grace in our lives and suggests that we save ourselves through our own good works. In a talk that the pope gave to priests and members of consecrated life, he said, "Two principles for you who are priests and consecrated persons: every day renew the conviction that everything is a gift, the conviction that your being chosen is gratuitousness—we do not merit it—and every day ask for the grace not to forget your memories, and not to fall into self-importance."[3] Francis's words are applicable not only to the lives of priests and consecrated persons but to every disciple of Jesus.

One essential way in which we experience God's grace is through the gift of forgiveness. In his apostolic exhortation on the Call to Holiness in Today's World, Pope Francis reflects on the Beatitudes, as found in the Gospel of Matthew (5:3–10). Commenting on the beatitude, "Blessed are the merciful, for they will receive mercy," Francis writes, "We need to think of ourselves as an army of the forgiven. All of us have been looked upon with divine compassion" (*Gaudete et Exsultate* 82). He likes to cite the reflections of Thomas Aquinas on mercy found in Aquinas's *Summa Theologiae*. There Aquinas argues that of all the virtues that have to do with our neighbor, mercy is the greatest. Aquinas names mercy as "something proper to God," and he asserts that it is through mercy, above all, that God shows forth God's almighty power.[4] For Aquinas, then, the power of the Creator of this unimaginably vast and ancient universe is manifested in the most compelling way in divine mercy. What a remarkable insight!

For Pope Francis, the first and primary word that the church must speak in its mission of proclaiming the gospel is the message about the mercy of God poured out in Jesus Christ. That truth is the heart of the gospel, and it is what people need to hear first. The pope's homily for the Mass for the Possession of the Chair of the Bishop of Rome was based on the parable of the prodigal son (Luke 15:11–32), which Francis names the "Parable of the Merciful Father." Reflecting on this famous gospel passage, Francis said, "The Son was always in the Father's heart, even though he had left him, even though he had squandered his whole inheritance, his freedom. The Father, with patience, love and mercy had never for a second stopped thinking about him." Then Francis added, "God is always waiting for us; he never grows tired."[5] In his 2015 Message for Lent, the pope urged Catholics to reflect the grace of God in our own lives by letting our hearts be formed into merciful hearts. And he immediately added that a merciful heart is not a weak heart. To become an authentically merciful person actually requires great inner strength.

In his apostolic exhortation The Joy of the Gospel, Francis applies this principle of the primacy of mercy to the celebration of the sacraments, especially the sacraments of reconciliation and the Eucharist. He reminds priests that "the confessional must not be a torture chamber but rather an encounter with the Lord's mercy which spurs us on to do our best." The pope proceeds to say, "A small step, in the midst of great human limitations, can be more pleasing to God than a life which appears outwardly in order but moves through the day without confronting great difficulties" (*Evangelii Gaudium* 44). About the Eucharist, the pope observes, "Although it is the fullness of sacramental life, [it] is not a prize for the perfect but a powerful medicine and nourishment for the weak" (no. 47). Both dimensions of that statement are important. The Eucharist is the fullness of sacramental life; it is the source and summit of the Christian life. At the same time, it is not a reward for those who are perfectly virtuous but a powerful medicine and nourishment for the weak—that is, for every Christian.

Pope Francis also echoes the Pauline message about reconciliation in his reflections on *communion*. In his encyclical on ecology, *Laudato Si'*, he describes the human person as a being who is "capable of self-knowledge, of self-possession and freely giving himself [herself] and entering into communion with others" (no. 65).[6] He proceeds to affirm that "as part of the universe, called into being by one Father, all of us are linked by unseen bonds and together form a kind of universal family, a sublime communion which fills us with a sacred, affectionate and inviolable respect" (no. 89). Human beings, then, are created for communion with God and with one another. And for Francis, *communion* is more like a verb than a noun. Communion is something that we must do; we are called to practice it. In a talk that he gave to a general audience in Rome, the pope said, "It is necessary to build communion, to teach communion, to get the better of misunderstandings and divisions, starting with the family, with ecclesial reality, in ecumenical dialogue, too. Our world needs unity; this is an age when we all need unity. We need reconciliation and communion, and the Church is the home of communion."[7] Francis continually urges us to transcend ourselves and our own small worlds in order to encounter and build communion with others. This mission includes the rebuilding of communion in relationships that have become strained or broken. It calls us to become a reconciled and a reconciling people.

A Gospel Story of Reconciliation

Robert Schreiter, a Precious Blood Missionary priest and theologian, has written extensively about the dynamics of reconciliation. He writes out of his keen awareness of processes of reconciliation that have been undertaken in countries where there has been considerable oppression and strife, such as South Africa, Chile, and Rwanda. His book titled *The Ministry of Reconciliation: Spirituality and Strategies*, is an informative and thought-provoking reflection on the dynamics of reconciliation and forgiveness.[8] Schreiter reads the gospel stories about the disciples' encounter with the risen Jesus as stories of reconciliation.

The appearances of the risen Christ become moments of recognition, reconciliation, and healing. With the help of Schreiter and other commentators, we can reflect on the encounter between the risen Christ and his disciples that is described in John 21. Scripture scholars conclude that this account was originally an independent narrative that was appended by an editor to the main body of the Gospel. It serves as an epilogue to the Gospel, especially in its characterization of the roles of Simon Peter and the beloved disciple.

> After this, Jesus revealed himself again to his disciples at the Sea of Tiberias. He revealed himself in this way. Together were Simon Peter, Thomas called Didymus, Nathanael from Cana in Galilee, Zebedee's sons, and two others of his disciples. Simon Peter said to them, "I am going fishing." They said to him, "We also will come with you." So they went out and got into the boat, but that night they caught nothing. When it was already dawn, Jesus was standing on the shore; but the disciples did not realize that it was Jesus. Jesus said to them, "Children, have you caught anything to eat?" They answered him, "No." So he said to them, "Cast the net over the right side of the boat and you will find something." So they cast it, and were not able to pull it in because of the number of fish. So the disciple whom Jesus loved said to Peter, "It is the Lord." When Simon Peter heard that it was the Lord, he tucked in his garment, for he was lightly clad, and jumped into the sea. The other disciples came in the boat, for they were not far from shore, only about a hundred yards, dragging the net with the fish.
>
> When they climbed out on shore, they saw a charcoal fire with fish on it and bread. Jesus said to them, "Bring some of the fish you just caught." So

Simon Peter went over and dragged the net ashore full of one hundred fifty-three large fish. Even though there were so many, the net was not torn. Jesus said to them, "Come, have breakfast." And none of the disciples dared to ask him, "Who are you?" because they realized it was the Lord. Jesus came over and took the bread and gave it to them, and in like manner the fish. This was now the third time Jesus was revealed to his disciples after being raised from the dead. (John 21:1–14)

We can imaginatively enter into this story of revelation and reconciliation. After the terrifying trauma of Good Friday, the disciples are mysteriously back in Galilee. They have returned to the occupation they had engaged in before they were called to follow Jesus. They have gone back to their familiar routine, or at least they are trying to do so. Schreiter points out that people who have been through great trauma "want to distance themselves as quickly as possible from the pain they have endured and the horrors they have seen."[9] This dynamic seems to be true of the disciples of Jesus as depicted in this narrative. The pain of Calvary, of Jesus's crucifixion, is still fresh and raw. But the attempt to distance themselves from all that has happened is futile. This futility is exemplified in the disciples' bad night of fishing. The Gospel puts it simply: "But that night they caught nothing." They are not getting anywhere in their attempt to return to the life they had before their encounter with Jesus.

Then they hear a mysterious voice coming to them from the lakeshore, addressing them as "Children." It is an affectionate address, even though the voice is at first unfamiliar. The risen Christ initiates the encounter. In the work of reconciliation, it is always God who takes the initiative. As we saw above, our own efforts at reconciliation are a response to divine grace. Whenever we have even the desire to be reconciled, that is already a sign of God's presence and loving action at work within us. And, as

Schreiter emphasizes in his reflections on the dynamics of reconciliation, it is usually the case that God begins the work of reconciliation in the lives of the victims.[10] God begins the process of reconciliation by restoring to victims of harm and injustice a sense of their own personal dignity. In this Gospel scene, the victim is Jesus himself: subjected to an unjust, brutal death; the victim of betrayal and denial by his closest followers; but raised to new life by the Father. He is the one who calls out to his disciples and so begins the process of leading them into a new future.

The disciples do not recognize Jesus at first. Nevertheless, they heed his word by casting their net to the starboard side. They must have wondered what good that would do. But it is after they do what he tells them that the beloved disciple can recognize who it is that is calling them. Sometimes the paths that we think we should follow are not the ways of God, and we need to try something different. The disciples will not discover new life after the crucifixion of Jesus by returning to their former occupations or by trying to ignore the pain they feel from all that has taken place. They must come face-to-face with the Lord and discover in their encounter with him the healing and the hope that they need.

And so they make their way from the boat to the shore, with Peter impetuously jumping into the water to race to the risen Christ. One must wonder what Peter expected would be the response that Jesus would give him. What would Jesus say to this man who had denied being Jesus's disciple at his moment of greatest need? When Peter and the others reach the shore, they discover that the risen Christ is acting as their host, preparing a meal for them. Their initial experience of him is one of hospitality. For reconciliation to happen, there must be an atmosphere of safety and hospitality.[11] Jesus provides such a safe haven on the lakeshore.

Jesus begins to converse with Peter beside the charcoal fire. Earlier in the Gospel, after Jesus had been arrested, Peter had stood outside the courtyard of the high priest next to another charcoal fire. When asked whether he was a disciple of Jesus, he had insisted, "I am not" (John 18:25). But something completely different will take place next to the charcoal fire lit by the risen Christ. The narrative continues:

> When they had finished breakfast, Jesus said to Simon Peter, "Simon, son of John, do you love me more than these?" He said to him, "Yes, Lord, you know that I love you." He said to him, "Feed my lambs." He then said to him a second time, "Simon, son of John, do you love me?" He said to him, "Yes, Lord, you know that I love you." He said to him, "Tend my sheep." He said to him the third time, "Simon, son of John, do you love me?" Peter was distressed that he had said to him a third time, "Do you love me?" and he said to him, "Lord, you know everything; you know that I love you." [Jesus] said to him, "Feed my sheep. Amen, amen, I say to you, when you were younger, you used to dress yourself and go where you wanted; but when you grow old, you will stretch out your hands, and someone else will dress you and lead you where you do not want to go." He said this signifying by what kind of death he would glorify God. And when he had said this, he said to him, "Follow me." (John 21:15–19)

Three times Jesus asks Peter, "Do you love me?" Is Jesus rubbing salt in the wound by repeating this question? Is there a tone of accusation in the air, repeating the question three times to match Peter's threefold denial? It seems, rather, that this rhythmic repetition of the question is Jesus's strategy of calling forth the love that Peter has always had for Jesus. Schreiter likens this threefold questioning by Jesus to the power of ritual in the work of healing and reconciliation. The three questions "constitute a ritual way of undoing Peter's three denials of Jesus."[12] Jesus knows well that Peter really does love him, despite his failure in a moment of crisis. And so Jesus acts to draw out the love that Peter has for him—to evoke it and bring it to expression.

It seems a bit strange that in this Gospel narrative Jesus does not explicitly tell Peter that he forgives him. One might think that would be the case. Instead, Jesus's forgiveness of Peter is implied in the reconnection that he makes with Peter. It is also evident in Jesus's entrusting Peter with a mission of leadership in the community: "Feed my lambs; tend my sheep." Through this commissioning, Jesus assures Peter that he trusts him. What a terribly risky thing for Jesus to do! Jesus entrusts Peter with the care of his followers, despite his proven weakness and fragility. Peter is called once more to follow Jesus and to shepherd his people. Just as Jesus is the Good Shepherd who lays down his life for the sheep (John 10:11), so Peter, faithful unto death, will become the pastor of Jesus's followers.

Becoming a Reconciled and Reconciling People

In their encounter with the risen Christ the disciples received the gift of forgiveness and peace even before they asked for it. Out of that transformative experience they were empowered to become ambassadors of the reconciliation about which Paul speaks in his Second Letter to the Corinthians. Every Christian, too, is summoned by Christ to be an instrument of God's grace in healing relationships, in breaking down the walls that separate people from one another. To become an ambassador of reconciliation, we need to return to Christ again and again to be reconciled with him ourselves. We need to step back, take an honest look at our lives and our relationships, and seek the Lord's mercy for the ways in which we have not responded to his call to love.

It seems that one challenge to this vocation of reconciliation is that of harboring resentment. Resentment, of course, can be a normal human reaction to experiences of injustice, betrayal, or violence from others. It is normal to feel resentment when others have hurt or disappointed us in a significant way. There are some things in life that we should resent. And the call to live as reconciling people does not mean that we ignore the hurt or disappointment we have experienced. The familiar maxim urging us to "forgive and forget" can trivialize the pain that someone has experienced, and it overlooks the fact that there are some harmful experiences that are never forgotten. The grief and anger that accompany such experiences need to be expressed; they must have their day in court. As Schreiter puts it, "In forgiving, we do not forget; we remember in a different way."[13] We choose not to be bound by the past. Through the grace of reconciliation, our memory is shaped by the perspective of God, who is the source of healing for all the wounds that we inflict on one another. Even though the scars from our wounds often remain, the grace of reconciliation enables us to move on toward the future without being held bound by the wounds of the past.

There are times, however, when we cling tightly to the resentment we feel. It becomes a source of negative energy in our lives. I know that I have a "terrorist" running around inside of me. He looks just like me. He tends to kidnap the people who hurt or disappoint me and to hold them as prisoners. He holds them in the prison of my heart as hostages of my resentment. This dynamic usually takes place before I even know it is happening. Christ must knock very loudly to remind me to untie those people and to let them go free. It is only through our willingness to free the hostages of our resentment over and over again that we can discover freedom for ourselves.

A few years ago, I heard a radio interview with former President Bill Clinton. The interview focused on Clinton's interactions with the late Nelson Mandela, the former President of

South Africa, who survived many years of harsh imprisonment under an apartheid regime. Clinton mentioned that he once asked Mandela whether, when he was finally freed from prison, he felt hatred for the government leaders, guards, and others who were involved in his imprisonment. Clinton said that Mandela admitted that he did feel hatred for them at first. But as time went on, he realized that if he continued to harbor hatred for them, they would, in his words, "still have me." He would remain their prisoner if he let himself be consumed by hatred. Mandela's words illumine the truth that we experience inner freedom when we can free the inner hostages of our resentment and hatred.

Perhaps when we hear gospel passages about the command to forgive, we imagine that forgiveness is an act that can be accomplished instantaneously. Or that it is a "state" that we simply fall into. We can confuse the will with the emotions. Forgiveness and efforts at reconciliation are acts of the will; they involve decisions that we make. They are not always feelings, at least at first. Often the positive feelings associated with forgiveness and reconciliation come only later, even much later. Forgiveness is a process comprised of small steps, of little acts of the will. It can begin with the simplest of prayers: "Lord, help me to learn how to forgive that person." Or even, "Lord, help me to want to forgive that person." Often, we need to ask even for the desire to forgive. We can be confident, however, that such prayers are always answered by the God who in Christ was reconciling the world to Godself.

One of the quandaries that we face in trying to become reconciling people is the situation where the other person (or persons) is not open to reconciliation, whoever was at fault in the first place. What does one do when there is no response from the other person, or even no apparent interest in resolving a disagreement or healing a wound? Many misunderstandings and disputes in our lives remain unresolved. We are often left with loose ends in the work of reconciliation. What we can do, however, is to strive to forgive the other person and to be freed from the grip of resentment. And we can pray that God will give that other person whatever grace he or she needs in their life. We can pray for the well-being of that person, with as much sincerity as we can muster. Often that is the first step in the process of reconciliation. And sometimes that is all that we can do. But in itself it is a momentous step and a powerful tool in the work of reconciliation. Praying for another person with whom we are struggling is not magic, but it can help us to see them differently, to see them a little more the way that God sees them.

Gazing on the face of Christ the Good Shepherd invites us to become instruments of his reconciling work in the world. In a world where difference and resentment often degenerate into polarization and hatred, followers of Jesus are called to proclaim by our lives that in Christ God was and is reconciling the world to Godself. We who have experienced God's abundant mercy in our own lives are, like Paul, commissioned to become ambassadors of reconciliation for Christ.

FOR REFLECTION

- Reflect on the ways in which you have experienced God's mercy and forgiveness in your life. How has that experience inspired you to show mercy to others?
- Call to mind someone from whom you feel distant, or with whom you have been in conflict. Pray for that person, asking God to give them the grace that they need in their lives and to help you better understand them.

Chapter 6

Christ, Priest and Brother

Every Christian—indeed, every human being—grapples with the experience of suffering in her or his life. As we listen to news of world events and as we reflect on our own lives and those of the people we love, we soon realize that suffering is not a problem to be solved but a mystery that exceeds our comprehension. Theologian Edward Schillebeeckx (1914–2009) remarked about this realization in one of his important works on Christology. Schillebeeckx wrote, "Thus, suffering and evil can provoke a scandal; however they are not a *problem*, but an unfathomable, theoretically incomprehensible *mystery*."[1] Not even the most astute philosopher or theologian can construct a rational framework that encompasses and justifies the "barbarous excess"[2] of human suffering that has scarred human history.

Christians turn to the person and destiny of Jesus to find meaning and hope in the suffering they encounter. As we saw in the second chapter, the healing ministry of Jesus was an integral dimension of his proclamation of the reign of God. Jesus had firsthand experience of people who suffered terribly, and his healing presence brought new life and hope to them. In times of struggle and suffering, we are also drawn to the foot of the cross and there meet the crucified one in his final agony. We meet the Divine Brother in distress. In the passion narrative found in the Gospel of

John, the crucified Christ gives the beloved disciple to his mother and his mother to the beloved disciple (John 19:25–27). In the act of giving his beloved disciple to his mother, he makes this disciple, and all his beloved disciples, his brothers and sisters.

In living with the mystery of suffering, I believe that we are invited to gaze on the face of Christ who is our Priest and our Brother. In the New Testament, the title of "priest" for Jesus is not common. It is, however, a title that is very prominent in the Letter to the Hebrews. Apparently, the author of this letter thought that this title for Jesus fit well with the argument he was crafting to encourage a disheartened community of Christians who had faced hardship and opposition for their faith and were growing weary of living the demands of the Christian life. They were tempted to give up on the Christian way of life and return to their former allegiances. And, in a somewhat more implicit way, we catch a glimpse of the priesthood of Christ near the end of the lengthy farewell discourse in the Gospel of John. There we listen as Jesus utters the "High Priestly Prayer" for his disciples and for those who will believe in him in the future (John 17). It is a beautiful and compelling passage that speaks to us of the continuing activity of Christ the Priest in the life of the church and in the life of each individual believer.

Throughout these passages, especially in the Letter to the Hebrews, Christ can be called *Priest* because he is *Brother* to those who follow him. He can exercise his unique, eternal priesthood on our behalf because of his *solidarity* with us. And so we turn our gaze to Christ who is Priest and Brother.

Christ the Compassionate High Priest

The Letter to the Hebrews is an intriguing book of the Bible. Its authorship is not certain. The great third-century scripture scholar and theologian Origen of Alexandria concluded that only God knows who wrote Hebrews. The letter is more of an extended sermon addressed to a community of Christians, possibly a community of Jewish Christians, who had grown discouraged in their faith because of the difficulties that Christian discipleship had brought them. New Testament scholar Daniel Harrington suggests that Hebrews may have been addressed to a group of Jewish Christians living in Rome in the sixties of the first century, during the reign of the emperor Nero.[3] The main message of the letter is that Jesus Christ is both the perfect sacrifice for sins and the great High Priest who freely offered himself for sinners. This image of Christ the Priest became particularly important in later Christian theology and liturgy. In making his argument, the author relates the suffering that the community has experienced to the suffering of Jesus. In so doing, he emphasizes that Christ can be our Priest because he became our Brother and is our Brother. Christ is the Priest who is our Brother.

The Letter to the Hebrews strongly affirms the unique, divine identity of Jesus. At the very beginning of the letter, the author speaks of Christ as the Son through whom God created the universe. Christ is the refulgence of the glory of God, the very "imprint" of God's being (Heb 1:2–3). As Son, Jesus is higher than the angels, and he accomplishes a salvation that is matched by no one else. This letter became an important biblical text for the Christian affirmation of the divinity of Jesus and for the development of the doctrine of the incarnation.

At the same time, the author of Hebrews stresses that Jesus can be our High Priest because he is one of us; he is our Brother, like us in his humanity in every way except for sin. His likeness to us enables him to serve as mediator of salvation. Unless Jesus was truly one of us, he could not be the Priest who accomplished our salvation by offering himself. In and through Jesus, then, God acted to save and offer life not by sweeping in from on high with the heavenly "armies" to vanquish his enemies and conquer the world. Rather, in Jesus, God acted to save by plunging into our human condition, even with all its messiness, pain, and suffering. This means that Jesus the High Priest truly experienced the suffering that wounds humanity and creation. He came face-to-face with the scourge of suffering in his own life and in the lives of those to whom he ministered. In the second chapter of Hebrews, the author writes, "For it was fitting that he, for whom and through whom all things exist, in bringing many children to glory, should make the leader to their salvation perfect through suffering" (Heb 2:10). He adds, "Therefore, he is not ashamed to call them 'brothers'" (Heb 2:11). A few verses later, the author proceeds to affirm of Christ that "he had to become like his brothers [and sisters] in every way, that he might be a merciful and faithful high priest before God to expiate the sins of the people. Because he himself was tested through what he suffered, he is able to help those who are being tested" (Heb 2:17–18).

This letter, then, presents us with a picture of Christ as fully sharing our humanity, even sharing in the human experience of temptation and suffering. In speaking about the priesthood of Jesus, Hebrews highlights his solidarity with us. Two other passages in the letter express this truth in a very compelling way. They are worthy of sustained reflection:

> Therefore, since we have a great high priest who has passed through the heavens, Jesus, the Son of God, let us hold fast to our confession. For we do not have a high priest who is unable to sympathize with our weaknesses, but one who has similarly been tested in every way, yet without sin. So let us confidently approach the throne of grace to receive mercy and to find grace for timely help. (4:14–16)

> Son though he was, he learned obedience from what he suffered; and when he was made perfect, he became

the source of eternal salvation for all who obey him, declared by God high priest according to the order of Melchizedek. (5:8–10)

The Letter to the Hebrews assures us, then, that as the great High Priest, Christ identified and continues to identify with us in our humanity, especially in the struggles and suffering that mark human existence. Jesus's own vocational pathway involved passing through the human experience of suffering. That was the journey that enabled Christ to become the source of eternal salvation for all who obey him. Reading this letter recalls a well-known saying of Pope Francis. Francis emphasizes the need for priests and other pastoral ministers to know and to be close to the people they serve. The shepherds should be so close to the sheep that they have the "smell of the sheep." Christ the Good Shepherd—Priest and Brother—took on the smell of the sheep. Thus he is forever close to us.

Some years ago, I visited an elderly man in his nineties who was confined to a nursing home. I had come to know him over the years and visited him often. He was in a typical nursing home room that had two beds; he spent most of his day in bed. On one day, I noticed that on the wall directly across from his bed, above the bulletin board, someone had mounted a crucifix. I commented to him that I had not noticed it there during my previous visits. He said to me, "Yes, I asked the nurse to hang that crucifix there. I know that I am probably going to die here in this bed, and I want that crucifix to be the last thing I see before I die."

His words made an impression on me, and I reflected on them as I drove away from the nursing home that day. It seemed clear to me that he saw in the crucified Jesus a sign, a sacrament, of the depths of God's love for us. Gazing on the crucified Christ, he discovered someone who could identify with him and with whom he could identify, as he spent the final days of his life. He seemed to realize that the crucified and risen Christ—the great

High Priest of the Letter to the Hebrews—was in solidarity with him. This was the Christ who was able to sympathize with his weaknesses. He saw in the crucified Christ his Brother, and he wanted that crucifix to be the last thing he would see before he died. He wanted to make his death a dying *with Christ*.

The Compassion of Christ in the Christian Tradition

The theme of the compassion of Christ, so eloquently articulated in the Letter to the Hebrews, has also been expressed in compelling ways in the Christian spiritual and theological tradition. Among the authors who have addressed it are Saint Augustine (354–430), Pope Saint John Paul II (1920–2005), and Pope Benedict XVI. Each of these thinkers offers us important insights as we grapple with the mystery of suffering.

Augustine. Besides being a brilliant theologian, Augustine was also the bishop of a busy seaport city who manifested a deep concern for the pastoral needs of the people he served. Ministering in North Africa in the first part of the fifth century, he was keenly aware of calamitous events that caused suffering for many people, including the sack of Rome in 410 and the invasion of his own city of Hippo by the Vandals in 430, during which Augustine died. Augustine wrestled with the mystery of evil and suffering throughout his life, from his early days as a seeker of the truth. And as a pastoral leader, he took the reality of human suffering with utmost seriousness. He keenly realized that people needed to experience the compassion of Christ in their lives.

Augustine's perspective on the nature of the church aided him in his reflection. For Augustine the church is first and foremost the Body of Christ. He focused on the New Testament image of the church as Christ's Body. Augustine, along with other early

Christian theologians, liked to speak of the "Whole Christ"—the *totus Christus*. The church is one reality composed of Christ the head of the Body intimately united with all believers who comprise the rest of the Body. This meant that for Augustine there is an indescribably close union between Christ and the church, which also entails a union between Christ and every believer.

Augustine draws upon this notion of the Whole Christ in some of his exquisite homilies on the psalms. He teaches that when the church prays the psalms it is the Whole Christ, head and members, that utters these prayers. He expresses this idea eloquently in a homily on Psalm 85:

> God could have granted no greater gift to human beings than to cause his Word, through whom he created all things, to be their head, and to fit them to him as his members. He was thus to be both Son of God and Son of Man, one God with the Father, one human being with us. The consequence is that when we speak to God in prayer we do not separate the Son from God, and when the body of the Son prays it does not separate its head from itself. The one sole savior of his body is our Lord Jesus Christ, the Son of God, who prays for us, prays in us, and is prayed to by us. He prays for us as our priest, he prays in us as our head, and he is prayed to by us as our God.[4]

For Augustine, when the church prays, Christ is praying for us, Christ is praying in us, and Christ is prayed to by us. Our prayer and Christ's prayer are intertwined, wrapped up in one another. Augustine appeals to this principle when he comments on the laments, the many psalms in the Bible that express experiences of suffering, often with arresting honesty and boldness. In commenting on these psalms, Augustine accentuates the closeness of Christ to the suffering members of his Body. Like the Letter to the Hebrews, Augustine underlines the solidarity of Jesus with every suffering person. Augustine proposes that, just as the earthly Jesus prayed the psalms during his life, so the risen Christ prays *in* those believers who cry out to God in lament:

> Accordingly, when we hear his voice, we must hearken to it as coming from both head and body; for whatever he suffered, we too suffered in him, and whatever we suffer, he too suffers in us....This solidarity meant that when Christ suffered, we suffered in him; and it follows that now that he has ascended into heaven and is seated at the Father's right hand, he still undergoes in the person of the Church whatever it may suffer amid the troubles of the world, whether temptations, or hardship or oppression.[5]

Augustine's deep conviction about the profound union between Christ and the church led to his compelling reflections on the intimacy and solidarity that exist between Christ and every suffering member of Christ's Body. This is the Christ that the Letter to the Hebrews presents as our compassionate High Priest, as offering loud cries and tears to the one who was able to save him from death and who was heard because of his reverence. The Jesus who cried out in lament in the garden of Gethsemane is indescribably close to every suffering member of his Body.

John Paul II. This image of Christ in the closest possible union with the suffering members of his Body is also found in the writings of Popes John Paul II and Benedict XVI. In 1984, John Paul II wrote an important letter that was titled "On the Christian Meaning of Human Suffering" (*Salvifici Doloris*).[6] In that letter the pope offered an intricate analysis of the experience of suffering in its many different forms. During his reflections, John Paul mentions the "why" question that people inevitably ask when they or someone they love are afflicted with serious suffering:

"Why is this happening? Why is this happening to me—or to that person I love so much? What is the reason for this?" Most people have asked that question at some point in their lives.

Pope John Paul affirms that "God expects the question and listens to it" (*Salvifici Doloris* 10). As the many psalms of lament in the Bible testify, God does not reject us when we complain about suffering or ask probing questions. The pope proceeds to say that the suffering believer soon discovers that the one to whom he or she addresses this "why" question is himself suffering. The one who responds to our queries and pleadings about suffering is the crucified Christ. He answers us from the cross, from the heart of his own suffering. John Paul says that the "answer" that Christ gives is not a theoretical explanation. Rather, it is a call to follow—an invitation to discipleship. It is an invitation to the suffering person to unite her or his suffering with the cross of Christ. The pope echoes Augustine in identifying the church as the Body of Christ. He writes, "In this body, Christ wishes to be united with every individual, and in a special way he is united with those who suffer" (no. 24).

Benedict XVI. In his second encyclical letter, "On Christian Hope" (*Spe Salvi*),[7] Pope Benedict XVI also took up this theme of the relationship of Christ to suffering people. He reflects on the experience of suffering in light of the hope that Christ offers us. Like the Letter to the Hebrews, Augustine, and John Paul II, Benedict highlights the solidarity of Christ with every suffering person. He quotes the testimony of a nineteenth century Vietnamese martyr, Paul Le-Bao-Tinh, who chronicled both the horrors of his imprisonment and his own unshakeable faith amid torment. Benedict observes, "Christ descended into 'Hell' and is therefore close to those cast into it, transforming its darkness into light" (*Spe Salvi* 37). The pope puts "hell" into quotation marks, suggesting that it refers to many forms of suffering and desolation, in this life and beyond. This is a remarkable affirmation about the presence of the crucified and risen Christ in all the deathly places of human experience, even to the very depths of those who seem to be lost. Benedict says that Christ travels to the farthest regions of darkness to be with those who are suffering. The pope finds in this remarkable truth of faith a challenge to all who believe in Christ. He speaks of the Christian vocation to become bearers of consolation to others. As he puts it, this consolation—*con-solatio* in Latin—suggests being with the suffering person in his or her solitude, so that it ceases to be solitude (no. 38). And Benedict affirms that it is God himself who is the ultimate bearer of this consolation.

Pope Benedict quotes a statement by the great Cistercian abbot and theologian of the twelfth century Bernard of Clairvaux. Bernard said that though God is impassible (immune from suffering), God is not "incompassible." Benedict expresses it this way: "God cannot suffer, but he can suffer with" (*Spe Salvi* 39). The pope proceeds to say, "Man [*sic*] is worth so much to God that he himself became man in order to *suffer with* man in an utterly real way—in flesh and blood—as is revealed to us in the account of Jesus's passion. Hence in all human suffering we are joined by one who experiences and carries that suffering *with* us; hence *con-solatio* is present in all suffering, the consolation of God's compassionate love—and so the star of hope rises" (no. 39).

Christ the Intercessor

A second dimension of the role of Christ as Priest and Brother that is portrayed in the Letter to the Hebrews is the intercessory prayer of Christ. The author of the letter says that because the crucified and risen Christ remains forever, he has a priesthood that does not pass away: "Therefore, he is always able to save those who approach God through him, since he lives forever to make intercession for them" (Heb 7:25). As one who became our Brother, like us in his humanity in all things except sin, he knows our experience from the inside and is always with us and for us in prayer. We often make this affirmation about Christ's intercession in the prayers of the liturgy, for example, when we confess in the penitential rite, "Lord Jesus, you intercede for us at the right hand of the Father."

This intercessory prayer of Jesus is also recounted at the end of the farewell discourse in the Gospel of John. The Fourth Evangelist sets this discourse at the Last Supper, prior to the commencement of Jesus's passion. Just before the Evangelist narrates the arrest of Jesus, he recalls the prayer of Jesus for his disciples: "I pray for them. I do not pray for the world but for the ones you have given me, because they are yours, and everything of mine is yours and everything of yours is mine, and I have been glorified in them" (John 17:9–10). In his prayer, Jesus recalls his care for and protection of the disciples: "When I was with them I protected them in your name that you gave me, and I guarded them" (John 17:12). And then Jesus expands the scope of his prayer, saying, "I pray not only for them, but also for those who will believe in me through their word, so that they may all be one, as you, Father, are in me and I in you, that they also may be in us, that the world may believe that you sent me" (John 17:20–21). He prays for unity among all who believe in him; he asks that God may be known in and through the unity of his followers. And he prays that his followers may make God known just as he has made God known. Jesus and the disciples share a mission to make God known in the world. Jesus is keenly aware of the fragility of his disciples and the momentous challenges they will face. As their Priest and Brother, he offers all who believe in him to the Father, so that God's presence and care may embrace and strengthen them.

Our belief in Christ's intercession for us is essential as we face the challenges of discipleship in the contemporary world. We may not think of Christ's intercession very often. We are more accustomed to invoking the intercession of Mary and the saints. This priestly image of Jesus the Intercessor is a fraternal image, a brotherly one. It connotes solidarity and accompaniment along the journey of discipleship. Jesus, Priest and Brother, Intercessor, is the Christ who is *for us*—always for us, praying for the best for us and praying for the best in us.

Bearers of Consolation

Some years ago, I visited a young couple whom I had known for a long time. Their oldest child was in a hospital intensive care unit just a few days away from his death. David was born with a rare neurological disorder. He managed relatively well for the first couple of years of his life, but when he was just three years old, he suffered a severe stroke. The stroke left him almost completely incapacitated. For four years, his parents, Joan and Bill, took exceptional care of David, until he died at the age of seven. They accompanied him with exquisite care and remarkable compassion. In his final days, when I visited them at the hospital, they never left David's side. Despite the profound sadness of the situation, I found their attentiveness to their son to be a source of inspiration. Like all parents who lose a beloved child, they have grieved deeply since his death. But the compassion that they showered on their son was a compelling example to all who knew them. They were living examples of what Pope Benedict means when he speaks of our call to become "bearers of consolation" to one another. They showed their son the face of Christ, who is our compassionate Priest and Brother.

Canadian theologian Phil Zylla authored a book titled *The Roots of Sorrow*, in which he developed a pastoral theology of suffering.[8] He explores what the Christian tradition says about the mystery of suffering, referring often to his experience and that of his wife of being parents to a daughter who was born with spina bifida and had to undergo many surgeries as a child. Throughout his book Zylla emphasizes that *compassion* does not always come easily or naturally to us. He argues that we are more naturally inclined toward a stance of *indifference* when we encounter people who are suffering. He contends that one of the key invitations for Christians is to make the move from a stance of indifference to one of compassion. Zylla's contention is not unlike what Pope Francis has often said when he laments the "globalization of indifference." Zylla asserts that a compassionate response to others means "to move into the suffering of others with active help."[9] We are called to move *into*—rather than *away from*—the suffering of others whom we meet.

When I first read Zylla's book, I reacted to his claim about the human inclination toward indifference. I like to assume that human beings have a natural aptitude and impulse for compassion. Nevertheless, Zylla's challenging observations are worthy of reflection. It is often more comfortable for us to remain in a stance of indifference toward others than to move into their pain. We sometimes hear people speak of "compassion fatigue." This phrase has even entered our national rhetoric regarding our attitude toward migrants and refugees from impoverished or war-torn nations. And in dealing with others in our own families and communities, we may discover that we are indeed prone to compassion fatigue. Pope Benedict's call to become bearers of consolation to others requires commitment and perseverance. It is often easier to show the compassion of Christ to the people one encounters in ministry or in professional work than to family or community members whom we know in a more personal way. Our awareness of the foibles of those we know more personally can make it more challenging to offer an attentive, compassionate presence to them. Nevertheless, the Lord Jesus, our compassionate Priest and Brother, invites us again and again to reveal his face to those who are sharing in his passion in their lives.

We are invited, then, to gaze on the face of Christ, who is our compassionate Priest and Brother. Recalling the words of the Letter to the Hebrews, we come before the High Priest who can sympathize with our weaknesses, and thus we can approach the throne of grace to receive mercy and to find grace for timely help. We remember, too, the reflections of Augustine about prayer: when we turn to Christ in times of sorrow it is Christ who is praying for us, Christ who is praying in us, and Christ who is prayed to by us. Having encountered the boundless compassion of Christ in our own lives, we are sent forth to become bearers of consolation to others.

FOR REFLECTION

- In what ways have you experienced the compassion of Christ through others in your life? What impact did that experience have on you?
- Do you think of yourself as "naturally" compassionate, or as more inclined toward indifference?
- Who are the people in your life for whom you are called to be a "bearer of consolation"?

Chapter 7

Christ the Prince of Peace

In this chapter we continue to take a long, loving look at the reality of Jesus Christ. We do so as disciples of the Lord who are committed to peace. The gospel call to walk with Christ entails a commitment to live in peace with ourselves and with others and to serve as peacemakers in the world. Jesus names peacemakers "blessed," and he promises that they will be called "children of God" (Matt 5:9). And so, we move from reflecting on Christ as Priest and Brother to gazing on Christ the Prince of Peace.

Whenever I preside at the celebration of the Eucharist, two of the prayers at the liturgy that speak to me very directly immediately follow the recitation of the Lord's Prayer. I usually find myself vocalizing these prayers with particular emphasis. In the first, the priest says, "Deliver us, Lord, we pray, from every evil, graciously grant peace in our days, that, by the help of your mercy, we may be always free from sin and safe from all distress as we await the blessed hope and the coming of our Savior, Jesus Christ." And in the following prayer the priest directly addresses Christ: "Lord Jesus Christ, who said to your Apostles: Peace I leave you, my peace I give you, look not on our sins, but on the faith of your Church, and graciously grant her peace and unity in accordance with your will." As the years have gone by in my ministry as a priest, these prayers have come to be very significant to me, and I connect them closely with the meaning of the Eucharist.

In the Letter to the Colossians, Paul (or the Pauline author of this letter) enumerates a list of virtues in which the Christians should "clothe" themselves. He exhorts these believers to exhibit compassion, kindness, humility, gentleness, and patience. And then he says, "And let the peace of Christ control your hearts, the peace into which you were also called in one body" (Col 3:15). The peace of Christ is something to which those who comprise the Body of Christ in the world are called. The peace of Christ is a kind of "vocation" within the Christian vocation. It lies at the heart of the Christian vocation. Ultimately, this peace is a gift from Christ, the Prince of Peace.

Knowing that we are called to live in the peace of Christ is inspiring and encouraging, yet many believers have difficulty in actualizing this teaching in their lives. Even when I pay special attention to the prayers of the Eucharist just cited, I find it to be a formidable challenge to internalize Christ's gift of peace. We live in a fast-paced, rapidly changing, and stress-filled world. It is difficult not to allow that stress to get inside of us. We extol the capacity to "multitask;" applicants for jobs highlight their ability to multitask on their resumes. Often when I teach theology, even graduate theology, I have to remind my students to put away their cell phones unless they need them for something that directly pertains to the class. Despite that reminder, some students cannot resist the temptation to text their friends during class. I also see people texting when crossing a busy Chicago street, sometimes while pushing a baby stroller at the same time. It seems that we are very often trying to do three things at once.

We also live in a world that is plagued by violence. Every evening, the broadcasts of the national and local news set this violence before our eyes, whether it is the gun violence that afflicts our city streets or the various arenas of international conflict around the globe. The scourge of violence has even struck our schools, taking the lives of innocent children. It is difficult to fathom the fact that elementary and high school students now must conduct regular drills to prepare for an active shooter on the school premises. The drumbeat of violence that we see and hear on the news, and sometimes up close, has a way of getting inside of us after a while. Peace is a precious and rare commodity in the contemporary world. Heeding the call of the Letter to the Colossians to allow the peace of Christ to control our hearts remains an abiding challenge for all of us.

Cardinal Joseph Bernardin and the Gift of Peace

When I gaze on the face of Christ the Prince of Peace, I am reminded of the book written by the late archbishop of Chicago, Cardinal Joseph Bernardin (d. 1996)—*The Gift of Peace*.[1] In this gem of a book, Cardinal Bernardin reflected on the journey of what were the final years of his life. During those years, he was faced with the onset of cancer and with a false allegation of sexual abuse by a former seminarian. *The Gift of Peace* is filled with wisdom about life with God, especially about living within the peace of Christ.

Writing about his arduous journey through surgery and postoperative treatment for cancer, Bernardin says that he prayed to God for the grace to handle those experiences without undue bitterness or anxiety. He observes, "God's special gift to me has been the ability to accept difficult situations, especially the false accusation against me and then the cancer. His special gift to me is the gift of peace."[2] Further along in the book, after receiving the news that his life expectancy was less than one year, Bernardin recalls what he said to the news media about the situation: "While I know that, humanly speaking, I will have to deal with difficult moments, I can say with all sincerity that I am at peace. I consider this as God's special gift to me at this moment in my life."[3]

In thinking about Cardinal Bernardin's personal testimony, I have wondered what it was that he did to create an openness within himself to receive Christ's gift of peace throughout the tumultuous final period of his life. If peace is Christ's farewell gift to us (see John 14:27), then we need to be open enough to receive that gift. We need to fashion within ourselves a receptivity to the gift of peace. Three recurring themes in Bernardin's book stand out for me: his commitment to personal prayer; his effort to let go of things he could not control; and his desire for reconciliation. It seems that these commitments, which Bernardin made and kept, paved the way for his reception of Christ's gift of peace at the end of his life. I believe that these same commitments also pertain to us in fashioning a receptivity to Christ's gift of peace.

Commitment to Personal Prayer

Cardinal Bernardin offers a very honest account of the challenge that some of his diocesan priests presented to him while he was bishop of Cincinnati. He recalls that at the time he was not setting aside adequate time for personal prayer. He writes, "It was not that I lacked the desire to pray or that I had suddenly decided prayer was not important. Rather, I was very busy, and I fell into the trap of thinking that my good works were more important than prayer."[4] At a dinner with three priests, two of whom he had ordained, Bernardin shared some of his difficulties with personal prayer. The priests were quite honest in their responses, telling him that he was urging a spirituality on others that he was not fully practicing himself. They went on to challenge him to set aside quality time for prayer. As a result of that conversation, Bernardin decided to give

God the first hour of each day, in order to be present to God in prayer and meditation so that he could open the door ever wider to God's entrance into his life. He recalls that this practice put his life into an entirely new and uplifting perspective.

Throughout his book Bernardin returns to this theme of personal prayer again and again. It is a leitmotiv of his book. He describes how difficult it was for him to pray after his surgery. He wanted to pray but, like many who suffer from illness, he found himself too distracted with the physical discomfort to do so. He told friends who visited him in the hospital, "Pray while you are well, because if you wait until you're sick you might not be able to do it."[5] He describes the way in which his regular prayer in the morning helped him to stay connected with the Lord throughout the remainder of the day. Bernardin encourages his readers to "keep plugging away" at prayer even when it does not seem to be going well. He observes that "if you do give the time, little by little you become united with the Lord throughout your life."[6] He then proceeds to say, "Without prayer, you cannot be connected or you cannot remain united with the Lord. It's absolutely essential."[7]

Mature Christians are accustomed to hearing exhortations about the importance of prayer. In some ways, it is "standard fare." Such advice is so familiar that we can easily become deaf to it. But in my own journey of faith and ministry, I have slowly realized the wisdom and essential importance of advice about prayer like that offered by Cardinal Bernardin. And I have noticed that when I fail to give adequate attention to prayer in my own life, my chances of experiencing Christ's gift of peace decrease significantly. While prayer is not a "magical potion," there seems to be a direct correlation between a deeper life of prayer and a deeper experience of peace.

We can build on Bernardin's observations and explore the insights of three other thinkers who can be helpful in deepening our understanding of personal prayer. The first is the great twentieth-century German theologian Karl Rahner, whom we have already encountered in this book. The second is the popular spiritual writer Bishop Robert Morneau. And the third is Pope Francis.

Often when we do take time for prayer, we find it difficult to attend to what we are doing. I find that to be the case in my own life, particularly when I am being pressed by multiple demands. I become easily distracted. Karl Rahner addresses that experience in his book *On Prayer*.[8] This spiritual classic is based on a series of Lenten sermons that Rahner delivered at a church in Munich, Germany, in 1946—less than a year after the end of the Second World War. Rahner was asked to preach a Lenten mission to a parish community, and he chose the topic of prayer. It is difficult to imagine what the parishioners must have been feeling at the time, as they were trying to recover from the trauma of a brutal war and were beginning to grapple with the horror and shame of the Nazi atrocities.

In his sermons Rahner evokes an experience that must have been imprinted on the memories of the parishioners. He refers to their experience of fleeing to air raid shelters when their city was being bombed during the war. After the explosions, the people would emerge from the shelters covered with debris. Rahner says, "Let this be taken as the symbol of modern life." He suggests that we often find our hearts to be obstructed, buried beneath all the rubble of life.[9] We frequently find our hearts to be covered with debris.

I find Rahner's image of the rubbled-over heart to be illuminating. This "rubble" can consist of many things: the worries and anxieties that flood our minds; experiences of disappointment and suffering, which can leave our hearts hardened or even embittered; the resentments that we harbor because of the ways that others have treated us. When we come to God in prayer, we need to ask God to set our hearts free. We must invite God to clear away the rubble that covers our hearts and minds so that we can be free enough to attend to God's presence with openness and love.

Sometimes our time of prayer becomes an exercise of worrying in the presence of God. We remain fixated on a particular problem or simply preoccupied with all that we need to do. At other moments our hearts are rubbled-over with feelings of disappointment or resentment, and we forget to ask the Lord to clear away the debris and to set our hearts free. Rahner's advice about praying for the grace of freedom is essential for receiving Christ's gift of peace. We must continually ask God to liberate our hearts.

Bishop Robert Morneau proffers ten basic principles to guide people in their prayer.[10] The centerpiece of Morneau's principles of prayer is deceptively simple. He writes, "In prayer I must bring this me to the living and true God."[11] We might call this the "honesty principle" of prayer. It actually forms the foundation of genuine prayer. Morneau observes, "To play a role in the presence of the Lord prohibits encounter at the deepest level of our being. To demand perfection flowing from the ideal self only leads to guilt. God invites us to come as we are, in our grace and our sin."[12]

Knowing that we are invited to come to the living and true God as we are can be a liberating discovery. It can also be a daunting challenge at times, even for people who are experienced in prayer. This truth is liberating because it is grounded in our belief in God's compassion; as the Letter to the Hebrews puts it, Christ is our compassionate High Priest. It is freeing because we come before the God who knows us through and through and takes us as we are. A close reading of the Gospels assures us that when anyone came to Jesus sincerely seeking his help, he never sent them away. He never said, "Go home; get your life straightened out, and then we will talk." He always took the person where they were and helped them to move to the next step in their journey to God. So our belief that we can bring "this me" to the living and true God is grounded in the life and ministry of Jesus.

At the same time, this honesty principle can also be challenging for us because sometimes it is difficult to come before God as we are. For any number of reasons, we may be inclined to try to conceal aspects of ourselves and our lives from the Lord, even though we are aware that it is impossible to do that. If we are haunted by the gut feeling that we will never quite measure up—if that is the "default position" of our psyches—we will find it too risky to share our real selves with anyone, even with God. If we think that we can bring ourselves to the living and true God only after we have addressed all our personal problems, we will never get there. To become a person of prayer, it is essential to speak to the Lord as honestly as possible about everything that is going on in our lives. Cardinal Bernardin's spiritual testament reflects the honesty of his own conversations with the Lord. And that was one of the keys to his realization of the gift of peace in his life.

Pope Francis has often spoken about the importance of prayer for the life of every Christian. He envisions a church that is contemplative. In *The Joy of the Gospel* he emphasizes that the evangelizing work of the church must be fueled and sustained by prayer. Francis observes, "What is needed is the ability to cultivate an interior space which can give a Christian meaning to commitment and activity" (no. 262).[13] He employs strong language to underline his point: "Without prolonged moments of adoration, of prayerful encounter with the word, of sincere conversation with the Lord, our work easily becomes meaningless: we lose energy as a result of weariness and difficulties, and our fervor dies out" (no. 262). The words about prayer that Francis originally addressed to a group of catechists gathered in Rome are particularly compelling. The pope told the catechists about a young man who had approached him and explained that, while he was very happy to meet the pope, he did not have the gift of faith. Francis did not berate him or chide him for his lack of faith. Rather, he urged the young man not to become discouraged, and he assured him of God's love for him. Then he suggested that the young man should let himself be gazed upon by God. Francis then proceeded to say to the catechists, "And this is the same thing I would say to you: let yourselves be gazed at by the Lord."[14] He spoke similar words to a group of priests about prayer before the Blessed Sacrament: "When we priests are before the tabernacle, and we pause there for a moment, in silence, we then feel Jesus's gaze upon us once more; this gaze renews us, reinvigorates us."[15] Francis's invitation to allow ourselves to be gazed upon by the Lord reflects his vision of a church that is contemplative. His words also open a way to experience Christ's gift of peace in our lives.

Letting Go

Cardinal Bernardin begins *The Gift of Peace* with a section that he titles "Letting Go." And the challenge of letting go, of learning to entrust himself more fully into the hands of God, permeates his reflections throughout the book. He admits that this was an ongoing struggle for him, as it is for all of us. Bernardin remarks, "Still, letting go is never easy. I have prayed and struggled constantly to be able to let go of things more willingly, to be free of everything that keeps the Lord from finding greater hospitality in my soul or interferes with my surrender to what God asks of me."[16] In a reflection on the mystery of suffering, he says that "our participation in the paschal mystery…brings a certain *freedom*: the freedom to let go, to surrender ourselves to the living God, to place ourselves completely into his hands, knowing that ultimately he will win out! The more we cling to ourselves and others, the more we try to control our destiny—the more we lose the true sense of our lives, the more we are impacted by the futility of it all."[17] Bernardin suggests that "it is in the act of abandonment that we experience redemption, that we find life, peace and joy in the midst of physical, emotional and spiritual suffering."[18]

After Bernardin found out that his cancer had returned and

was inoperable, he presided at a communal celebration of the sacrament of the anointing of the sick in a suburban Chicago parish. He told the people gathered for the liturgy that they must place their lives completely into the hands of the Lord. As he put it, "We must believe that the Lord loves us, embraces us, never abandons us (especially in our most difficult moments). This is what gives us hope amid life's suffering and chaos."[19]

Despite the evident wisdom of Bernardin's remarks, many people, including me, find it quite difficult to let go of the things that we cannot control in life. The motto by which some of us tend to live is this: "It's never too soon to start worrying." I often find it very difficult to place everything into the hands of the Lord, especially when I am faced with multiple demands and responsibilities. But the Lord has ways of slowly teaching us these things, often through the people he places in our lives. For me one of those people was a young adult who participated in a summer conference for Catholic young adults that I directed a few years ago. John had been an excellent athlete in high school and was on his way to play football in college. But on the day of his high school graduation, he dove into his family's aboveground pool, hit the bottom, and suffered a severe spinal cord injury that left him paralyzed from the waist down. He uses a motorized wheelchair and drives a specially equipped van. Having now graduated from college, John teaches at a high school.

John has a wisdom and sense of self-possession that are far beyond his years. At the opening session of the summer conference, there was the usual icebreaker in which participants were asked to talk with the person sitting next to them and then introduce that person to the entire group. Each person stood as they introduced their partner. When the time came for John to introduce his partner, he put the entire group at ease by simply saying, "I think I'll stay seated for this one." Our group encountered several mobility challenges throughout the week at the sites we visited. Some of the venues were not as accessible as we had been led to believe, making it awkward and embarrassing for John and for us. But John never seemed to become flustered by any of it. He just took it in stride and made the best of it. I was amazed at the serenity that he exhibited throughout the week, even amidst unexpected and difficult circumstances. He seemed to be a young man who was at peace. I believe that Christ taught me something about letting go through this inspiring young adult.

The ability to entrust our lives and our projects to Christ frees us to live emotionally and spiritually healthy lives. It enables us to take time for rest, for the Sabbath time that each of us needs. Psalm 127 is a beautiful prayer that serves as a healthy reminder for all who have difficulty letting go of their work and its results:

> Unless the LORD build the house,
>   they labor in vain who build.
> Unless the LORD guard the city,
>   in vain does the guard keep watch.
>
> It is vain for you to rise early
>   and put off your rest at night,
> To eat bread earned by hard toil—
>   all this God gives to his beloved in sleep. (vv. 1–2)

The ability to let go enables us to recognize that maintaining relationships with significant people in our lives is essential, no matter how busy we may be. Those relationships help to keep us human and whole. The willingness to let go also makes possible the necessary detachment from the results of our endeavors. For those who minister in the church, this means that ministry does not become "all about us." The familiar adage attributed to Mother Teresa of Calcutta can sound a bit hackneyed, but there is genuine wisdom in it: the Lord does not call us to be successful but to be faithful. Letting go of success—however we define success—is terribly difficult at times. It does not entail approaching our work in a haphazard or unprofessional manner. But we know well that we often have little control over the results of our efforts. The willingness to let go instills in us a certain freedom and peace. Cardinal Bernardin's insight into the importance of letting go forms an enduring dimension of his witness to the gift of peace that he received from Christ.

The Desire for Reconciliation

Cardinal Bernardin's well-known meeting with the man who falsely accused him of sexual abuse points us to a third dimension of his experience of the gift of peace. He writes about his desire to meet with Steven Cook after the accusation had been retracted and the legal case withdrawn. He said: "I felt deeply that this entire episode would not be complete until I followed my shepherd's calling to seek him out. I only prayed that he would receive me. The experience of false accusation would not be complete until I met and reconciled with Steven."[20]

When they finally met, Bernardin told Steven that he had prayed for him every day and would continue to pray for his health and peace of mind. In reflecting on their experience of celebrating the anointing of the sick and the Eucharist together, Bernardin says, "Never in my entire priesthood have I witnessed a more profound reconciliation. The words I am using to tell you this story cannot begin to describe the power of God's grace at work that afternoon. It was a manifestation of God's love, forgiveness and healing that I will never forget."[21] Bernardin related this event to the work of the Good Shepherd: "to seek and restore to the sheepfold the one that has been, only for a while, lost."[22]

We explored the theme of reconciliation in chapter 5. There I mentioned the important work of Robert Schreiter on reconciliation and forgiveness. Schreiter observes that, while reconciliation requires concrete strategies that are effective, it is more of a spirituality than a strategy. Reconciliation is about something much deeper than technique. As he states it, "If reconciliation is principally God's work, then we are but 'ambassadors for Christ' (2 Cor 5:20)."[23] Schreiter speaks of building communities of reconciliation; such communities "are places where memory can be recovered, a memory that is redemptive of the suffering of the past and not a continuing destroyer of persons and communities."[24] Communities of reconciliation are also communities of hope, where a common future can be built together.

It appears that what Schreiter says about the spirituality of reconciliation was evident in the life of Cardinal Bernardin. He became an ambassador for Christ in his outreach to Steven Cook, as well as to many other people. And his desire for reconciliation was an essential dimension of his finding peace in his life. Each of us is invited to embrace the spirituality of reconciliation of which Schreiter speaks. This is an approach to life and to other people that seeks to heal and unite rather than retaliate and divide. A spirituality of reconciliation motivates us to strive for liberation from the chains of resentment. It is on the lookout for possibilities of dialogue where there has been misunderstanding. It searches for common ground where positions and perspectives appear to be irreconcilable. The spirituality of reconciliation impels believers to create communities where the grace of forgiveness is the "atmosphere" within which they live and relate to one another.

At the end of *The Gift of Peace*, Bernardin offers these remarks: "What I would like to leave behind is a simple prayer that each of you may find what I have found—God's special gift to us all: the gift of peace. When we are at peace, we find the freedom to be most fully who we are, even in the worst of times. We let go of what is nonessential and embrace what is essential. We empty ourselves so that God may more fully work within us."[25] Cardinal Bernardin's path to receiving Christ's gift of peace included three personal choices: his commitment to personal prayer; his effort to let go of things he could not control; and his desire for reconciliation with others, including the man who very nearly ruined his life. I suggest that our own path to the peace of Christ entails these same three choices. And Bernardin is certainly correct in his final observation: when we are at peace, we find the freedom to be most fully who we are as disciples of the Lord.

> Lord Jesus Christ,
> who said to your Apostles:
> Peace I leave you, my peace I give you,
> look not upon our sins,
> but on the faith of your Church,
> and graciously grant her peace and unity
> in accordance with your will.
> Who live and reign forever and ever.
>
> Order of Mass, Communion Rite

For Reflection

- What does Christ's gift of peace mean in your life?
- How can you experience Christ's peace more deeply by strengthening your commitment to personal prayer, by letting go of things you cannot control, and by striving for reconciliation in your relationships?

Chapter 8

Christ the Good Samaritan

The Prince of Peace who offers us the gift of peace and calls us to live in his peace is also the Lord who sends us forth. Christ commissions us to continue his mission of proclaiming the reign of God in the world today. Pope Francis has repeatedly taught us that every baptized Christian is called to be a "missionary disciple"—a follower of Jesus who is "sent forth" to the world to embody and to announce the good news of God's saving love poured out in Jesus Christ. And we know from personal experience that the world to which we are sent is a wounded world, where the crucified of today await the compassion of Christ.

The parable of the Good Samaritan is a gospel passage that has spoken to believers through the centuries about who Christ is, his relationship with us, and the mission that he hands on to us. It is, I believe, an instructive and illuminating word of Scripture with which to conclude our exploration of the multiple dimensions of the mystery of Christ. Of course, for most of us, the story is so familiar that we can easily become deaf to its true meaning and power. The words of Jesus's parable can pass right over our heads. But if we listen to it closely, it can make a lasting impact on us, as it must have done for those who first heard Jesus tell the story.

> There was a scholar of the law who stood up to test [Jesus] and said, "Teacher, what must I do to inherit eternal life?" Jesus said to him, "What is written in the law? How do you read it?" [The lawyer] said in reply, "You shall love the Lord, your God, with all your heart, with all your being, with all your strength, and with all your mind, and your neighbor as yourself." [Jesus] replied to him, "You have answered correctly; do this and you will live."
>
> But because he wished to justify himself, [the lawyer] said to Jesus, "And who is my neighbor?" Jesus replied, "A man fell victim to robbers as he went down from Jerusalem to Jericho. They stripped and beat him and went off leaving him half-dead. A priest happened to be going down that road, but when he saw him, he passed by on the opposite side. Likewise a Levite came to the place, and when he saw him, he passed by on the opposite side. But a Samaritan traveler who came upon him was moved with compassion at the sight. He approached the victim, poured oil and wine over his wounds and bandaged them. Then he lifted him up on his own animal, took him to an inn and cared for him. The next day he took out two silver coins and gave them to the innkeeper with the instruction, 'Take care of him. If you spend more than what I have given you, I shall repay you on my way back.' Which of these three, in your opinion, was neighbor to the robbers' victim?" He answered, "The one who treated him with mercy." Jesus said to him, "Go and do likewise." (Luke 10:25–37)

Christct the Good Samaritan

The setting for this parable is introduced by two questions from an expert in the Law of Moses—the sacred Torah. Luke tells us that he posed these questions to Jesus to test him. In the context of Luke's Gospel narrative, this scholar of the Law is depicted as trying to trap Jesus. Biblical scholar Dianne Bergant comments about this scholar and his questions: "In a very real sense the lawyer is asking the right question, but his reason for asking is wrong: to catch Jesus in some error."[1]

Bergant is perceptive in suggesting that the lawyer is asking the right question. His question, "What must I do to inherit eternal life?" reflects a query and a longing that lie deep within our souls, too. It evokes the quest for wholeness—for integrity—that we find deep within us, even if we do not articulate this desire in the same words found in the Gospel. It points us to our search for how to live in right relationship with God and with others.

The lawyer adds a second question as well: "And who is my neighbor?" Luke tells us that he addressed this second question to Jesus because he wanted to justify himself. Bergant suggests that he poses this second question to Jesus to "save face."[2] Perhaps, however, the lawyer was like people we know who need to have life tied up in a neat package, or clearly marked out with bold lines. We know people who have high control needs and who, therefore, have trouble dealing with ambiguity, with the many "gray areas" of life. Or, perhaps like many of us, the lawyer simply felt overwhelmed by the needs in his world and knew that he could not respond to all of them. Don't we often have the same "overwhelmed" feeling? We cannot respond to all the requests for assistance that we receive in the mail, many of them very worthwhile. So the lawyer wants his duties and obligations precisely specified so that he will be able to proceed with a sense of certitude.

In response to these questions, Jesus tells this scholar of the Law a parable, a story that many of us know by heart. It is a "nice" story about a good deed. The term *Good Samaritan* has even made its way into our everyday parlance. We call the person who

95

stops to help the tire changer by the roadside or who offers a meal to a homeless person a Good Samaritan. There are Good Samaritan laws that protect physicians and other health care providers who stop to assist people in medical emergencies.

New Testament scholar Luke Timothy Johnson observes, however, that "the parable is intended to provoke."[3] This story would not have sounded so nice to the scholar of the Law or to many of Jesus's contemporaries. The lawyer and other listeners may well have been thinking, "Jesus, how can you possibly tell a story about love of neighbor in which the hero is a Samaritan? Don't you know what those people are like?" Indeed, there was a history of very bad blood between Samaritans and Jews. They disagreed about the right place to worship (Mount Gerizim vs. Mount Zion), the correct way to interpret the sacred books, and the question of who was a real Israelite.[4] And this rivalry had at times become very violent. For the Jews of Jesus's day, the Samaritans did not worship correctly or observe Torah properly. Moreover, the Samaritan should not have been traveling on this road from Jerusalem to Jericho in the first place. He is "at risk in this dangerous no man's land of deserted territory," and he increases that risk by stopping to help the wounded man.[5] Amy Jill Levine, a prominent Jewish scholar of the New Testament, likens this Gospel story to a modern parable that would feature an Israeli Jew lying in a ditch on the West Bank; the person who stops and shows him compassion is a member of Hamas.[6]

Jesus is clever and creative in the ways in which he weaves his provocative parables. He often turns things upside down. He does that with the lawyer's question, "And who is my neighbor?" In that question, "neighbor" refers to someone "out there" who should be the object of my love. But through the story that he tells, the word "neighbor" comes to mean someone "in here" — someone I become by way of action. The Samaritan becomes a neighbor through his compassionate response to the wounded victim. He becomes a neighbor through the way in which he "neighbors" the person in need.

The Greek word that is translated "moved with compassion" is the same term that is used to describe Jesus's reaction to the grief of the widow of Nain, who lost her only son (Luke 7:13), as well as the reaction of the father of the prodigal son when he sees his son returning (Luke 15:20).[7] It is also the term employed in the Gospel of Mark to depict Jesus's reaction to the sight of the leper who comes to him begging for help (Mark 1:41). In chapter 2, we saw that this term (*splagchnizomai*) connotes a visceral reaction, a being moved in one's "guts." Terrence Tilley suggests that it means something like, "his heart went out to him."[8] The response of the Samaritan to the sight of the wounded man in the ditch is like that of Jesus. The Gospel suggests that "the power of such compassion must be divine."[9] The Samaritan's compassion moves him to "approach" the victim, rather than to "pass by" on the opposite side as had the priest and the Levite before him.

In the early church, many famous teachers and preachers loved this gospel story, and they wrote extensively about it. These included the third-century theologian Origen of Alexandria; Jerome, the fifth-century scholar of the Bible; and Augustine, the fifth-century bishop of Hippo. In retelling this story, they gave a name to the fictional character of the Samaritan. They put a face on him. The name they gave to the Good Samaritan was Jesus Christ. They saw in this gospel character the face of their crucified and risen Lord. It is Jesus himself who is the first and the preeminent Good Samaritan.

This is the way in which Origen reflected on this gospel parable in one of his homilies on the Gospel of Luke.[10] He cites a tradition likening the man wounded and left for dead to Adam. Adam is wounded by the disobedience that is sin. The man lying by the roadside, then, represents a wounded humanity. The priest who does not stop to help represents the Law. The Levite symbolizes the prophets. Something, or someone, more powerful than the Law and the prophets is needed to heal a severely wounded humanity. The Samaritan, the one who stops and draws near, is the Son of God who became incarnate. As Origen puts it, "The Samaritan is that man whose care and help all who are badly off need."[11] Christ draws near to us to become our neighbor. Christ the Good Samaritan bears our sins and grieves for us. He brings the wounded man to the inn, which for Origen represents the church. The church is meant to receive all the wounded of our world. Origen proceeds to exhort his hearers to imitate Christ the Good Samaritan. He says, "We can go to them, bind their wounds, pour in oil and wine, put them on our own beasts, and bear their burdens."[12] In reflecting on Origen's homily, one is reminded of the image of the church often employed by Pope Francis—the church as a "field hospital" meant to receive and care for the wounded of the world. This image has deep roots in the theology and spirituality of the early church.

The image of Christ the Good Samaritan has been a formative one for me. I have a simple icon on the wall of my office. I look at it often and I find that it speaks to me about who Christ has been for me and who Christ calls me to be for others. The icon is a classic representation of this Gospel parable.[13] There is a man helping a wounded, bandaged victim onto a donkey. He is carefully lifting him up onto the animal. Off in the distance, one can see a small building at the end of the road—a cross between an inn and a church. The man who is lifting the bandaged victim has a halo. One quickly realizes that this man is Jesus. The Good Samaritan turns out to be Christ himself. Christ is the one who stops for us, stops for each one of us when we lie by the roadside in our need. He is the one who has drawn near to humanity in his incarnation to become our neighbor. And he remains neighbor at our side. It is the faithful Jesus, ever close to us, who is moved with compassion at the sight of each one of us. He approaches us, tends our wounds, and lifts us up.

The magnificent Chartres Cathedral in France is famous

for its stained glass windows. When it was built in the thirteenth century, ordinary Christians, many of whom could not read, were catechized in their faith through the stories told in the stained glass windows. One of those windows (the Good Samaritan Typological Window; Bay 44) reflects the early church's interpretation of the parable of the Good Samaritan. It depicts two classic biblical scenes joined together in a single window. First, it portrays the creation and the fall of Adam and Eve, complete with apple and serpent. Adam and Eve represent a wounded humanity — humanity in need of the compassion and healing of God. The window also depicts the Gospel story of the Good Samaritan. At the top of the window is the figure of Christ. The juxtaposition of these two biblical stories has the effect of portraying Christ himself as the Good Samaritan.

A Man Who Drew Near

On the street where I live in Chicago, at the Passionist residence across from Catholic Theological Union (CTU), there is a small apartment building. When I pass that building on my way to the store, I often see people sitting outside in their wheelchairs, especially if it is a warm summer day. It is an apartment building specially designed for persons with disabilities. Seeing these people makes me think of a Passionist priest who died of a brain tumor shortly after I was ordained — Flavian Dougherty. Flavian lived in our community at CTU when I was a seminarian. He had just finished ten years of service as the Provincial Superior of the Passionists, after which he decided to move to our community in Chicago. Flavian was one of those larger-than-life people we sometimes meet. He had a robust, enthusiastic personality, and he could light up a room with a story, a song (preferably "Frankie and Johnny"), or merely by his presence. He had been an all-city high school quarterback in Philadelphia, and he could have played college football, but he entered the seminary instead. He stayed in excellent physical condition, and he was quite a competitor. Playing tennis with Flavian was an exercise in "combat on the court."

After he moved to Chicago, Flavian became very involved with the community of persons with disabilities. He met with them regularly, and he listened to their concerns about life, society, and the church. He drew near to these people and he worked with them. He often spoke about how much he had learned from the wisdom of persons with disabilities, even how much they had taught him about God and his Christian faith. Along the way, Flavian joined with this community in advocacy work to secure their rights and well-being. He collaborated in efforts to convince the Chicago Transit Authority to provide more adequate bus service for persons in wheelchairs. He worked with others in proposing the construction of the apartment building down the street from CTU. Flavian persuaded pastors that it was appropriate (and important) for a person in a wheelchair or with braces to serve as a lector at the celebration of the Eucharist. And he helped to establish a pilgrimage to Israel for persons with disabilities.

Flavian never seemed to view his collaboration with persons with disabilities as a burdensome chore. Rather, he received new life and enthusiasm from his interaction and friendship with them. All his life, Flavian remained the "quarterback" leading his team down the field. But near the end of his life, it was another kind of endeavor in which he was engaged. When I pass by that apartment building, I can picture this healthy, energetic man sitting at a dinner table next to a person with a severe disability. I can see Flavian talking with her, listening to her, learning from her. Flavian was never able to bind up the wounds of these individuals; he knew that he could not remedy their disabilities, and he realized that they did not want him to do that, anyway. But he did know that he could approach these persons, listen with compassion, and allow himself to be taught by them. He could become neighbor to them. Flavian taught me about the meaning of the parable of the Good Samaritan.

Sent Forth

If we are attentive to the action of the Spirit in our lives, we come to recognize that Christ the Good Samaritan stops for us at those times when we are lying by the roadside. He is moved with compassion for us, approaches us, and tends our wounds. As I mentioned in chapter 2, the healing that Christ offers us is not magical. It is not like divine plastic surgery that makes the wounds in our lives simply disappear. It is not typically an instantaneous "fix." The healing that Christ the Good Samaritan offers us is the hope and the energy that enable us to move forward in life. It is the grace to keep going with the trust that Christ walks with us all along the way. Because of Christ, because of his faithful presence and compassion in our lives, we do not need to remain stuck, imprisoned in the past, fixated on the negative. We can move on with freedom.

From this experience of Christ's healing presence in our lives, each of us is commissioned to embody the compassion of Christ in the world. As I have mentioned, Pope Francis has consistently highlighted the missionary character of Christian life. Every baptized Christian is "sent forth" to proclaim the gospel of Jesus Christ by their words and by the example of their life. In the first chapter of his apostolic exhortation, *The Joy of the Gospel*, Francis recalls the biblical figures of Abraham, Moses, and Jeremiah, each of whom was told to "go forth" to accomplish the mission that God had entrusted to him. Francis asserts that "all of us are called to take part in this new missionary 'going forth'" (*Evangelii Gaudium* 20). He goes on to declare that an evangelizing community "gets involved by word and deed in people's daily lives; it bridges distances, it is willing to abase itself if necessary, and it embraces human life, touching the suffering flesh of

Christ in others" (no. 24). In his more recent exhortation, On the Call to Holiness in Today's World, the pope includes a section on discernment. He teaches that discernment "is not about discovering what more we can get out of this life, but about recognizing how we can better accomplish the mission entrusted to us at our baptism" (*Gaudete et Exsultate* 174). He proceeds to describe this personal discernment as "an authentic process of leaving ourselves behind in order to approach the mystery of God, who helps us carry out the mission to which he has called us, for the good of our brothers and sisters" (no. 175).

Pope Francis emphasizes that one dimension of this missionary vocation of the Christian entails expressing our solidarity with others. He has attempted to model this solidarity through actions like washing the feet of incarcerated persons on Holy Thursday and by traveling to places around the globe that have been scarred by protracted violence, like the Central African Republic and Colombia. Francis insists that Christians are called to "draw near"—to enter into solidarity with people who are suffering and marginalized in society. He admits that solidarity is viewed as a "bad word" by some people; for some it has Marxist connotations. In *The Joy of the Gospel*, Francis says that solidarity is poorly understood. It is something deeper than "a few sporadic words of generosity." Solidarity entails "the creation of a new mindset which thinks in terms of community and the priority of the life of all over the appropriation of goods by a few" (*Evangelii Gaudium* 88). In his encyclical On Care for Our Common Home (*Laudato Si'*), Francis extends this call to solidarity to our relationship with the natural world. Because of the ecological irresponsibility of human beings, the natural world itself has become like the man left by the roadside in the parable of the Good Samaritan. The pope urges us to recognize that "everything is interconnected, and this invites us to develop a spirituality of that global solidarity which flows from the mystery of the Trinity" (*Laudato Si'* 240).

We are commissioned to become mediators of Christ's

compassion to a church that is holy but has also been wounded by the horrific crimes of some of its ministers and by the failure of some of its leaders to respond to those crimes in an appropriate way. We Catholic Christians are part of a church that needs to be renewed and rebuilt. Our church is scarred not only by the sins of sexual abuse and financial misconduct. It is also wounded by the deep divisions among its members and the polarizing rhetoric that inhibits mutual dialogue. So we are summoned to be instruments of reconciliation within our church.

We live in a society in which bitterness and vengeance often seem to triumph over forgiveness. The rhetoric of many of our political leaders has a demeaning, degrading tone, which we have come to accept as "normal" political parlance. In our culture, too, it is all too easy to foster prejudice toward those who are different from us—bigotry toward the "Samaritans" in our society. The demonization of immigrants and refugees is one symptom of that attitude. We are sent forth to a society in which human life is threatened in all its stages, from conception until natural death. We live in a world where we seem to find it increasingly difficult and inconvenient to reverence the gift of human life. That is evident in the statistics about the number of abortions, the frequency of child and spouse abuse, the prevalence of gun violence on the streets of our cities, the sizeable populations of homeless persons in our cities, the threat faced by the poor and lower middle class of losing their health insurance, and the moves to legalize and sanitize assisted suicide.

The world in which we live is not a bad place. Our culture is not entirely corrupted. There is a wealth of beauty in the world—so much breathtaking beauty and profound goodness to behold. And there is much that is good and life-giving about the culture in which we live. Throughout the centuries, Christians have resisted the temptation to view the world in a purely negative light. Today, too, we need to recognize and to prize the goodness that is all around us in creation and within the people we meet.

At the same time, the world in which we live and work is also in need of Christ the Good Samaritan. And the hands of Christ the Good Samaritan are our hands. The compassionate gaze of Christ the Good Samaritan is offered to people through our eyes. Christ takes our hands and uses them to tend the wounds of those who have been left by the roadside in our world. Christ the Good Samaritan acts through us, as we learn what it means to become neighbor to those around us. Pope Francis's metaphor for the church as a field hospital strikes a chord with many people today living in a fractured world. Each of the baptized, each missionary disciple, has a role to play in helping the church to become a place of healing for people in need of it.

We are commissioned—sent forth—not as those who have it "all together"—those who are perfectly whole and have all the answers to life's mysteries. We are sent forth as those who bear the wounds of Jesus in our bodies and spirits. In the well-known phrase of the late Henri Nouwen, we are commissioned as "wounded healers." We are fragile disciples who continue to search and often to wrestle with our own fears, anxieties, and resentments. We are those empowered to stop for others who lie by the roadside because we have been there ourselves. The marvelous truth is that by becoming neighbor to those around us we discover healing and refreshment in our own lives.

> But a Samaritan traveler who came upon him was moved with compassion at the sight. He approached the victim, poured oil and wine over his wounds and bandaged them. Then he lifted him up on his own animal, took him to an inn and cared for him. (Luke 10:33–34)

Lord Jesus, risen with the wounds of your own crucifixion, you have been Good Samaritan to us; you have been neighbor to me. Show me how to become neighbor to those to whom you send me. Remind me to stop and not to rush on in haste. Give me your eyes to look with compassion on those in need. Give me your hands to tend the wounds of those who need to see you in seeing me. For I want to be friend to you, Jesus, and neighbor to them. Renew in me the grace of your friendship that will enable me to become neighbor to those around me.

FOR REFLECTION

- In what ways have you experienced Christ as the Good Samaritan in your own life? How has Christ stopped for you, lifted you up, and offered you healing and new life?
- How might Christ be calling you to become a neighbor to someone you know?

Epilogue

I began this book with a reference to the twentieth-century theologian Karl Rahner and his systematic theology. We saw that Rahner emphasizes that Christianity understands itself as a process of entering into a personal relationship with Jesus Christ. This process is an ongoing one that extends throughout a believer's life. Each person's relationship with Christ is unique, reflecting the particular context of her or his life. Rahner maintained that "in the individual Christian there must be a quite personal and intimate love for Jesus Christ." Each believer should be ready to throw his or her arms around the Lord.

The teaching of Pope Francis eloquently reflects this call to a personal relationship with Christ. Using the image of "gazing," Francis asserts that contemplation of the face of Jesus restores our humanity, even when our humanity has been wounded by sin or by some form of affliction. The pope insists that there is power in the face of Christ. There is power to heal and to offer life, even amidst the deathly experiences of life. Francis goes further to exhort Christians to allow the risen Christ to gaze upon them in prayer.

Throughout the previous chapters, we have reflected on some traditional christological titles, using them as windows through which to gaze on the inexhaustible mystery of the crucified and risen Jesus. Each window provides some insight into a dimension of the person of Jesus and his life-giving action in our lives.

So, Christ is friend, the one who called his disciples "friends" and who invites us to live in friendship with him. He is the friend who laid down his life for us. As Teresa of Avila said, Christ is true friend at our side. We are called to stay closely connected to him, to abide in him in a relationship characterized by mutuality. It is through entrusting our lives to Christ that we discover genuine freedom.

Christ is the healing presence of God, the one who was moved at the deepest part of his being when he saw the leper approaching him. He reached out to touch this "unclean" man and, in so doing, raised him from spiritual death. Christ announced the nearness of the reign of God and made God's reign present in the lives of those he encountered. And when Jesus made the gracious rule of God present, people found life, especially people who had had the life drained out of them in some way. In our own lives, even when a cure from affliction is not available, it is the compassionate presence of Christ that is the source of our deepest healing and our most enduring hope.

Christ is the one who calls women and men to follow him on the road of discipleship. He summons us to become people of ever-deepening faith, faith in the fullest sense of the term— confession, commitment, and confidence. And when our faith is little—anxious and hesitant—he reaches out his hand to lift us up, just as he rescued Peter from the terrifying abode of the deep and his paralyzing fear. In an increasingly secularized world, where living a life of discipleship does not receive the social support that it once did, Christ calls us to be people of courageous faith who are willing to make a personal decision to commit our lives to him.

Christ is the Bread of Life. He is the one who evokes and satisfies our deepest human hungers. He does this in a preeminent way through the gift of the Eucharist, the source and summit of our life as Christians. In the celebration of the Eucharist we discover who we are and whose we are—the one to whom we ultimately belong. And this Christ is ingenious in finding other ways to nourish us, to give us what we need so that we may continue to follow him on the journey of discipleship.

Christ is the Good Shepherd who goes in search of the one lost sheep. He is the one in whom God was and is reconciling the world to Godself. Risen and victorious over death, he came in search of Simon Peter by the lakeshore in Galilee. He knew that Simon Peter really did love him despite his failure in the crisis of Jesus's passion. So at the lakeshore, beside the charcoal fire, he acted to evoke Peter's love and bring it to expression. He is also the Christ who summons us to release the prisoners of our resentments—to set them free and in so doing discover freedom for ourselves. He calls us to become reconciled and reconciling people.

Christ is our Priest and our Brother, the one who can act as our compassionate High Priest because he became our Brother, like us in his humanity in every way but sin. Through Christ, God acted to save and to offer life by plunging into the human condition—even with its pain and suffering—to transform it from within. In his human life, Christ came face-to-face with the intractable mystery of suffering. So when the church prays its laments in times of tribulation, it is the risen Christ who is praying for us, Christ who is praying in us, and Christ who is prayed to by us. In the words of Augustine, whatever we suffer, he too suffers in us. Having experienced Christ's compassion, we are commissioned to become bearers of consolation to those who are suffering.

Christ is the Prince of Peace. In a fast-paced and often violent world, he calls us to live in his peace and to become peacemakers. He is the Lord to whom we can bring our real selves in prayer, knowing that he takes us where we are and enables us to move to the next step in our journey to God. He invites us to discover peace by letting go of what we cannot control and entrusting our lives ever more fully into his hands. And Christ summons us to make peace in the world by building communities of reconciliation, where a common future can be built together.

Christ is the Good Samaritan who has come to bring healing to a wounded humanity. He stops for us at those times in our lives when we are lying by the roadside. He is moved with compassion for us, and he tends our wounds. His healing presence enables us to move forward in life, not imprisoned in the negative dynamics of the past but able to move on with freedom. Christ is also the one who sends us forth to tend to the wounds of those who live by the roadside in our world. He acts through us as we learn to become neighbor to those around us.

And Christ reveals to us the beauty of God's face. As Augustine expressed it, Christ was beautiful in heaven and beautiful on earth, beautiful in the womb and beautiful in his parents' arms. He was beautiful even under the scourges because amidst the ugliness of his passion he disclosed the sublime beauty of infinite, self-giving love. We, then, are invited to gaze on the beautiful face of Christ and, in so doing, to discover new life.

Notes

PREFACE

1. Karl Rahner, *Foundations of Christian Faith: An Introduction to the Idea of Christianity*, trans. William Dych (New York: Crossroad, 1978/2013).

2. Rahner, *Foundations of Christian Faith*, 305.

3. Rahner, *Foundations of Christian Faith*, 308.

4. Rahner, *Foundations of Christian Faith*, 309.

5. Karl Rahner, *The Love of Jesus and the Love of Neighbor*, trans. Robert Barr (New York: Crossroad, 1983), 23–24.

6. Rahner, *The Love of Jesus*, 23.

7. The first part of this quotation is a citation of a talk given at a convention of Italian dioceses held in Florence in November of 2015. See *AAS* 107 (2015): 1284.

8. Joann Wolski Conn, "Spirituality," in *The New Dictionary of Theology*, ed. Joseph Komonchak, Mary Collins, and Dermot Lane (Wilmington, DE: Michael Glazier, 1987), 972.

9. Gerald O'Collins, *Jesus: A Portrait* (Maryknoll, NY: Orbis Books, 2008), 1–15.

10. Augustine of Hippo, *Exposition of Psalm 44.3*, in *The Works of Saint Augustine: A Translation for the 21st Century*, trans. Maria Boulding, OSB (Hyde Park, NY: New City Press, 2000), vol. III/16, 283.

11. O'Collins, *Jesus: A Portrait*, 10.

12. O'Collins, *Jesus: A Portrait*, 11.

13. O'Collins, *Jesus: A Portrait*, 15. *The Calling of Matthew* by Caravaggio can be found at https://images.app.goo.gl/7hdSkWz9nb8PsLMr9.

CHAPTER 1

1. Thomas Aquinas, *Summa Theologiae* II–II, 23, 1.

2. Teresa of Avila, *Life* 8, 5, in *The Collected Works of St. Teresa of Avila*, rev. ed., ed. Kieran Kavanagh and Otilio Rodriguez (Washington, DC, Institute of Carmelite Studies, 1987), 96.

3. Teresa of Avila, *Life* 22, 6, *The Collected Works*, 196.

4. Elizabeth Johnson, *She Who Is: The Mystery of God in Feminist Theological Discourse* (New York: Crossroad, 1992), 157–58.

5. Paul Wadell, "Friendship," in *The Collegeville Dictionary of Pastoral Theology*, ed. Carroll Stuhlmueller (Collegeville, MN: Liturgical Press, 1996), 349–53.

6. Wadell, "Friendship," 350.

7. Wadell, "Friendship," 350.

8. Gregory of Nazianzus, Oratio 14, *De Pauperum amore* 38, 40. Office of Readings for the Liturgy of the Hours, Saturday of the Third Week of Lent.

CHAPTER 2

1. Edward Schillebeeckx, *Church: The Human Story of God*, trans. John Bowden (New York: Crossroad, 1990), 111.

2. Walter Kasper, *Jesus the Christ*, trans. V. Green (New York: Paulist Press, 1976), 79.

3. Donald Senior, *Jesus: A Gospel Portrait*, rev. ed. (New York: Paulist Press, 1993), 116.

4. Raymond Brown, *An Introduction to New Testament Christology* (New York: Paulist Press, 1994), 64.

5. John R. Donahue and Daniel J. Harrington, *The Gospel*

of Mark, Sacra Pagina, vol. 6 (Collegeville, MN: Liturgical Press, 2002), 91.

    6. Donahue and Harrington, *The Gospel of Mark*, 89.

    7. Donahue and Harrington, *The Gospel of Mark*, 89.

    8. Pope Francis, "Spiritual Retreat Given by His Holiness Pope Francis on the Occasion of the Jubilee for Priests," Second Meditation, June 2, 2016, accessed March 30, 2020, http://w2.vatican.va/content/francesco/en/speeches/2016/june/documents/papa-francesco_20160602_giubileo-sacerdoti-seconda-meditazione.html.

CHAPTER 3

    1. See Donald Senior, *The Gospel of Matthew*, Interpreting Biblical Texts (Nashville: Abingdon Press, 1997), 63–70.

    2. Senior, *The Gospel of Matthew*, 64.

    3. John Meier, *Matthew*, New Testament Message 3 (Wilmington, DE: Michael Glazier, 1980), 165.

    4. Meier, *Matthew*, 165.

    5. Senior, *The Gospel of Matthew*, 129.

    6. Yves Congar, *A Gospel Priesthood*, trans. P.J. Hepburne-Scott (New York: Herder and Herder, 1967), 206–7.

    7. Gerald O'Collins, *Fundamental Theology* (New York: Paulist Press, 1981), 137–39.

    8. Karl Rahner, "The Spirituality of the Church of the Future," *Theological Investigations*, vol. 20, *Concern for the Church*, trans. Edward Quinn (New York: Crossroad, 1981), 149.

    9. Rahner, "The Spirituality of the Church of the Future," 149.

CHAPTER 4

    1. Francis Moloney, *The Gospel of John*, Sacra Pagina, vol. 4 (Collegeville, MN: Liturgical Press, 1998), 221–22.

CHAPTER 5

1. Jessica Powers, "The Mercy of God," *Selected Poetry of Jessica Powers*, ed. Regina Siegfried and Robert Morneau (Kansas City: Sheed & Ward, 1989), 21; quoted in Robert Morneau, *Reconciliation* (Maryknoll, NY: Orbis Books, 2007), 16–17.

2. Morneau, *Reconciliation*, 17.

3. Pope Francis, Meeting with Priests, Religious and Seminarians, National Marian Shrine of "El Quinche," Quito, Ecuador, July 8, 2015, in *Disciples Together on the Road: Words of Pope Francis for Priests* (Washington, DC: USCCB, 2016), 67.

4. Thomas Aquinas, *Summa Theologiae* II–II, q. 30, a. 4.

5. Pope Francis, Homily at the Mass for the Possession of the Chair of the Bishop of Rome, April 7, 2013, in *The Church of Mercy: A Vision for the Church* (Chicago: Loyola Press, 2014), 4.

6. Pope Francis, Encyclical Letter *Laudato Si'* (On Care for Our Common Home) (Vatican City: Libreria Editrice Vaticana, 2015), 65.

7. Pope Francis, General Audience, November 25, 2013; *The Church of Mercy*, 28.

8. Robert Schreiter, *The Ministry of Reconciliation: Spirituality and Strategies* (Maryknoll, NY: Orbis Books, 1998).

9. Schreiter, *The Ministry of Reconciliation*, 84.

10. Schreiter, *The Ministry of Reconciliation*, 14.

11. Schreiter, *The Ministry of Reconciliation*, 88.

12. Schreiter, *The Ministry of Reconciliation*, 92.

13. Schreiter, *The Ministry of Reconciliation*, 66.

CHAPTER 6

1. Edward Schillebeeckx, *Christ: The Experience of Jesus as Lord*, trans. John Bowden (New York: Crossroad, 1983), 725.

2. Schillebeeckx, *Christ*, 725.

3. Daniel Harrington, *Why Do We Suffer? A Scriptural*

Approach to the Human Condition (Franklin, WI: Sheed & Ward, 2000), 128.

4. Augustine of Hippo, *Exposition of Psalm 85, 1*, in *The Works of Saint Augustine: A Translation for the 21st Century, Expositions of the Psalms, III/18*, trans. Maria Boulding (Hyde Park, NY: New City Press, 2002).

5. Augustine of Hippo, *Exposition of Psalm 62,2*.

6. John Paul II, Apostolic Letter on the Christian Meaning of Human Suffering (*Salvifici Doloris*), February 11, 1984.

7. Benedict XVI, Encyclical Letter on Christian Hope (*Spe Salvi*), November 30, 2007.

8. Phil Zylla, *The Roots of Sorrow: A Pastoral Theology of Suffering* (Waco, TX: Baylor University Press, 2012).

9. Zylla, *The Roots of Sorrow*, 100.

CHAPTER 7

1. Cardinal Joseph Bernardin, *The Gift of Peace: Personal Reflections by Joseph Cardinal Bernardin* (Chicago: Loyola Press, 1997).

2. Bernardin, *The Gift of Peace*, 96.

3. Bernardin, *The Gift of Peace*, 135.

4. Bernardin, *The Gift of Peace*, 5.

5. Bernardin, *The Gift of Peace*, 67.

6. Bernardin, *The Gift of Peace*, 98.

7. Bernardin, *The Gift of Peace*, 100.

8. Karl Rahner, *On Prayer* (Collegeville, MN: Liturgical Press, 1993).

9. Rahner, *On Prayer*, 11.

10. Robert Morneau, "Principles of Prayer," in *Spiritual Direction: Principles and Practices* (Mahwah, NJ: Paulist Press, 1992), 11–28.

11. Morneau, "Principles of Prayer," 16.

12. Morneau, "Principles of Prayer," 17–18.

13. Pope Francis, Apostolic Exhortation on the *Joy of the Gospel* (*Evangelii Gaudium*).

14. Pope Francis, Address to the Participants at the International Congress on Catechesis, September 27, 2013, in *The Church of Mercy: A Vision for the Church* (Chicago: Loyola Press, 2014), 16.

15. Pope Francis, Speech Prepared by the Holy Father and Given during the Meeting with Diocesan Priests of the Cathedral (Cassano all' Jonio), June 27, 2014, in *Disciples Together on the Road: Words of Pope Francis for Priests* (Washington, DC: USCCB, 2016), 36.

16. Bernardin, *The Gift of Peace*, 6.

17. Bernardin, *The Gift of Peace*, 48.

18. Bernardin, *The Gift of Peace*, 48–49.

19. Bernardin, *The Gift of Peace*, 123–24.

20. Bernardin, *The Gift of Peace*, 34.

21. Bernardin, *The Gift of Peace*, 39.

22. Bernardin, *The Gift of Peace*, 40.

23. Robert Schreiter, *The Ministry of Reconciliation*, 16.

24. Schreiter, *The Ministry of Reconciliation*, 94.

25. Bernardin, *The Gift of Peace*, 152–53.

CHAPTER 8

1. Dianne Bergant, in Dianne Bergant with Richard Fragomeni, *Preaching the New Lectionary: Year C* (Collegeville, MN: Liturgical Press, 2000), 303.

2. Bergant, *Preaching the New Lectionary: Year C*, 303.

3. Luke Timothy Johnson, *The Gospel of Luke*, Sacra Pagina, vol. 3 (Collegeville, MN: Liturgical Press, 1991), 175.

4. Johnson, *The Gospel of Luke*, 162n53.

5. Johnson, *The Gospel of Luke*, 175.

6. Amy-Jill Levine, *Misunderstood Jew*, 148–49, cited in Terrence Tilley, *The Disciples' Jesus: Christology as Reconciling Practice* (Maryknoll, NY: Orbis Books, 2008), 159.

Notes

7. Bergant, *Preaching the New Lectionary: Year C*, 303.

8. Tilley, *The Disciples' Jesus*, 156.

9. Tilley, *The Disciples' Jesus*, 156.

10. Origen of Alexandria, Homily 34 on the Gospel of Luke, in *Origen: Homilies on Luke, Fragments on Luke*, Fathers of the Church, trans. Joseph Lienhard (Washington, DC: CUA Press, 1996), 137–41.

11. Origen of Alexandria, Homily 34 on the Gospel of Luke, in *Origen*, 139.

12. Origen of Alexandria, Homily 34 on the Gospel of Luke, in *Origen*, 141.

13. See https://images.app.goo.gl/wb588LGaHQjBGmPU8 (accessed April 8, 2020).